Write Better Stories and Essays:
Topics and Techniques to Improve Writing Skills for Students in Grades 6 Through 8

A Tool Kit For Young Writers

Write Better Stories and Essays: Topics and Techniques to Improve Writing Skills for Students in Grades 6 Through 8

Contributing Editor And Author	- George Smith
Contributing Editor	- Marisa Adams
Contributing Student Author	- Vivek M. Krishnaswamy
Designer	- Harini Nagaraj

ISBN-13: 978-1479142576

Printed in the United States of America

For permissions and additional information contact us

Lumos Information Services, LLC
PO Box 1575, Piscataway, NJ 08855-1575
http:/www.lumoslearning.com

Email: support@lumoslearning.com
Tel: (888) 408-1689
Fax: (866)283-6471

ABOUT THE AUTHOR

George Smith, a children's book author and publisher, has been conducting writing workshops at schools since 2004. He is passionate about helping young writers turn their creative story ideas to captivating stories that others would enjoy reading. He has authored two children's books, a marine life guide book for science teachers and functioned as an editor for several publications. He lives in Lakewood, New Jersey and loves to travel.

Table Of Contents		Page Number
	Introduction	2
I	Four Ways to Expand a Story Idea into a Story	3 - 9
II	Creative Techniques for Using Words and Paragraphs	10 - 20
III	Identifying Illogical or Incomplete Content, Inconsistent Voice (active or passive), Inconsistent Verb Tense (present and past) and Incorrect Grammar	21 - 24
IV	Expressing the Emotions of a Character: Show, Don't Tell!!	25 - 26
V	Using the Personification Technique	27 - 28
VI	Using the Flashback and Story Within a Story Techniques	29 - 35
VII	Using the Circular Text Technique	36 - 38
VIII	Using the Five Senses	39 - 41
IX	Using the Persuasion Technique	42 - 43
X	The Role of the Setting in a Story	44 - 48
XI	Presenting and Supporting Theories (Claims)	49 - 54
XII	Techniques in Action: Stories and Essays Written by Middle School Students	55 - 83
XIII	Answers	84 - 114
XIV	Common Core State Standards Initiative (CCSSI) Standards for Writing and Language	115-122
XV	Grading Rubrics For Exercises In Chapter I	123-127
	Online Resources	128

Introduction

The introduction of the Common Core State Standards into the American public school system has brought new opportunities and challenges to educators. It has created a conducive framework for raising the writing and reading skills of students across America. However, the classroom implementation of new standards is a challenging task since it requires translation of high level objectives and standards into something that students can relate to in a classroom setting.

The first objective of these workbook exercises is to give student authors practice in writing techniques that meet the standards for writing and language included in the Common Core State Standards Initiative (CCSSI), a state-led effort to establish national standards for students in the disciplines of reading, writing, speaking, listening and language. These standards are coordinated by the National Governors Association Center for Best Practices and the Council of Chief State School Officers. All of the standards that these workbook exercises support are listed in Chapter XIV. Within each chapter, the standards specific to that chapter are listed in the format CCSSI W(for Writing) or L(for Language) followed by the grade level and the paragraph number. Example: CCSSI W.6.3. Only those parts of the standard that relate to the exercise will be listed. In addition to displaying the standard that applies to each topic, we have included a recommended rubric for scoring the product that the student produces to meet the requirements of the standard

The second objective of these workbook exercises is to provide tools in the form of techniques that middle school student authors in grades 6 through 8 can use to improve the content of their narrative, persuasive, expository and descriptive writing.

Narrative writing communicates an author's experiences, either real or imaginary, over a period of time.

Persuasive writing presents an author's opinion or point of view, for the purpose of trying to influence or persuade a reader to agree with the author's opinion.

Expository writing provides information for the purpose of explaining a topic or giving directions.

Descriptive writing describes a character, setting and/or an event in such a manner that the reader can imagine that character, setting or event in their minds.

The third objective of this program is to create a platform for students to easily publish their writing online and get feedback from peers and educators. Writing is a skill that requires practice and mentoring. Students can become good writers through guided practice and constructive feedback. Please visit QuillPad.org to create an account and start publishing your stories and essays!

Online Resource: Publish and get feedback on www.QuillPad.org

I. Four Ways to Expand a Story Idea into a Story

Story Idea: A story idea is a short description of what a story will be about. It is usually written before the story is written. It may describe the primary plot, it may list or describe one or more characters, it may describe the relationships between characters and it may describe a setting. It only covers a few important details that will appear in the story; it is not the story itself. It may also include a description of the purpose of the story, for example, to inform, instruct, persuade, or entertain.

1. Plots

A plot describes the most important events and relationships in a story. An author can expand a story by increasing the number of events and/or the number of relationships in the plot, or by adding more details to events and/or relationships that are already in the plot. An author can also expand a story by adding additional primary plots (a primary plot is one whose events and relationships are most important to the author) and/or adding subplots (a subplot describes events and relationships that are not as important to the author as the primary plot is).

Events may be actions that characters take, or actions that affect characters. Actions that affect characters may be actions taken by other characters or by natural forces (ex. tornado or fire).

Relationships describe the way characters interact with other characters; the other characters may be other humans, supernatural beings, live plants or animals, or non-living characters.

Interactions between or among characters can take place at different levels. What do we mean by different levels? If an author writes about one character talking to another, or about an event that all characters are experiencing together, without any mention of what each character is thinking, that is a single level. It means that each character is completely aware of everything that is said or done. If the author adds what a character is thinking but not saying out loud, that is a second level, because the other character does not know what the first character is thinking. The same reasoning applies if two characters talk about another character and the other character is not aware of what was said. If a story includes the description of a dream, the dream is on a second level; the events in the dream are not taking place in the real world in which the dreamer lives.

2. Characters

An author can expand the length of a story by adding more information, such as physical descriptions, about existing characters, or by adding new characters with information about them. When an author adds a character, he or she is usually also adding an event that that character causes or participates in. *(Comment: Otherwise, why is the character in the story?)*

3. Setting

Setting refers to the location where an event or a relationship takes place, or to the time period in which an event or relationship takes place.

3.1 Location: An author can expand a story by describing the characteristics of the location of the setting and/or by adding additional settings.

3.2 Time Period: An author can expand a story by adding or changing time periods.

4. Graphics

Graphics refers to adding photographs, drawings, paintings, tables, charts or graphs to a story. Adding any of these will increase the length of a story.

Comment: These same techniques can be applied to a story published as a hard cover book or in digital form as a CD, DVD, tablet, movie or video

EXERCISES:

Below are three story ideas. Read each story idea and expand each using the four ways to expand a story described above in this chapter.

<u>Story Idea #1:</u> A Boat And Its Journey

Setting: a tidal river in the state of Maine
This story idea is about a small rowboat that is owned by a family and is tied to their dock.

After several days of rain, she fills with water and becomes so heavy that the wind and tide combine to snap her mooring line. She drifts down the tidal river, and as she drifts, she encounters various living and nonliving things typically found on a tidal river in Maine. Finally, she drifts into a cove on whose shore sits a house. A child of about 11 years old looks out the window of the house and sees the boat drifting toward their dock. Her family does not own a boat.

STUDENTS' WRITING ASSIGNMENT:

1. Write sentences or phrases describing how you would expand this story idea to a multi page story that would appeal to <u>elementary school students</u>. Assume this will be a picture book with story text. Use each of the four ways to expand a story that were described above in this chapter. You don't have to actually write the expanded story (unless you want to); you just have to describe the ideas you have for expanding the story.

_____
_____
_____
_____
_____

2. Include in the story at least one example of a marine life creature that would inhabit a tidal river in Maine, and explain how you were able to determine that this creature would live there.

_____
_____
_____
_____
_____
_____
_____

3. Which character or characters would tell the story and why did you choose them?

_____
_____
_____
_____
_____
_____

4. What title and subtitle (a subtitle is a short phrase that adds more detail to the actual title) would you give the story?

_____
_____
_____
_____
_____

Story Idea #2: An Amazing Chicken

Setting: _The area of the United States known as the Far West (includes states like Colorado, Arizona, New Mexico)._

A family of two parents and four children live in the Far West, on a two acre ranchette (a ranchette is a small ranch – just a couple of acres). They own a pig, several horses and ponies, goats, dogs, cockatoo birds, a rabbit and several hens. The family notices that one of the hens is very intelligent and friendly, and interacts with the other animals and with the family members. Because of these character traits, they give her a special name. They become very fond of her, and brag about her to all their friends.

SPIKE
The Amazing Chicken

STUDENTS' WRITING ASSIGNMENT:

1. Write sentences or phrases describing how you would expand this story idea to a multipage story that would appeal to <u>fifth and sixth graders</u>. You can assume this will have photographs with story text.

Use each of the four ways to expand a story that were described in this chapter. You don't have to actually write the expanded story (unless you want to); you just have to describe the ideas you have for expanding the story.

_____
_____
_____
_____
_____
_____
_____
_____
_____
_____
_____
_____

2. Who would you select to tell the story and why?

_____
_____
_____
_____
_____
_____

3. What title and subtitle (a subtitle is a short phrase that adds more detail to the actual title) would you give the story?

_____
_____
_____
_____
_____
_____

<u>Story Idea #3:</u> The Boy From Africa

<u>Settings</u>: *A poor country in Africa and a school and community in the U.S.*

You are a children's book author and you are looking for a new subject to write a book about. In the newspaper, you read an article about a teacher in an American school where many students are refugees from Liberia, an African country that has been involved in a civil war. This teacher is so moved by the sad stories that she hears from her students that she is determined to do something to help those left behind in the African country. Included in ways she is willing to help is the option of adopting an African child who is of elementary school age, since she does not have children of her own.

<u>*STUDENTS' WRITING ASSIGNMENT:*</u>

1. Write sentences or phrases describing how you would expand this story idea to a multipage story that would appeal to <u>middle school students</u>. You can assume this will be a picture book with story text.

Use each of the four ways to expand a story that were described in this chapter. You don't have to actually write the expanded story (unless you want to); you just have to describe the ideas you have for expanding the story

2. Explain how you would find out information about life in an African village in Liberia, to use in the story.

_____

_____

_____

_____

_____

_____

_____

_____

_____

_____

3. Who would you select to tell the story and why?

_____

_____

_____

_____

_____

4. What title and subtitle (a subtitle is a short phrase that adds more detail to the actual title) would you give the story?

_____

_____

_____

_____

_____

II. Creative Techniques for Using Words, Phrases, Sentences and Paragraphs

1. Avoiding redundancy within a story

This topic is designed to help authors recognize and eliminate words, phrases, sentences or paragraphs that are not necessary, because the reader can figure out the author's message without them. It also applies to an idea that has already been clearly expressed to the reader by the author, when expressing it again is not necessary (that is, it is redundant).

Example of redundancy: Many middle school authors overuse the words "then" or "next" when they are describing a series of events that occur sequentially (that is, one after the other). After describing the first event in a series of events, they think they have to begin every sentence that describes all the events that follow the first event with the words "then" or "next."

It is not necessary to use "then" or "next" if the author makes it obvious to the reader that these are a series of events happening sequentially, or when the author numbers the events in the order in which they occur (for example, the steps in a recipe). The reader understands that the events are in sequence and does not need to be reminded of this with the words "then" or "next."

EXERCISES:

In the following examples, there are redundant words, phrases and sentences. Draw a line through any word, phrase or sentence you think is redundant. Also, if you think a word, phrase or sentence needs to be added to make the meaning clearer, then give it a number, write it in the space provided below or on a separate piece of paper, and place that same number in the text where you think it should be inserted. The answers to Exercises 1.1 to 1.7 are in Chapter XIII. ANSWERS.

Exercise 1.1 "Maggi, come on good girl, wake up, come on, you have got to wake up!" Molly said. It was 8:00 in the morning and Molly was trying to wake up Maggi, her dog.

_____

_____

_____

_____

Exercise 1.2 "I have to call this lady and tell her that I found her dog and she can come and pick her up." Molly said, as she turned and walked slowly toward the phone. RING RING RING! rang the phone in Maggi's owner's house. "Good Morning. Carrie Lendwood speaking," said the lady on the other end of the phone.

_____

_____

_____

_____

Exercise 1.3 "Take a look at this dog collar." Molly said. Her mother took the collar from her hands and tried to read it, "The letters are too small. Hand me my reading glasses they are right there in the drawer," her mother said. Molly ran over to the drawer grabbed the glasses without even closing the drawer back ran back to her mother's side.

_____

_____

_____

_____

Exercise 1.4 An elderly women opened the door and screamed at the top of her weak lungs: "Oh my baby, where had you gone, your mother was furious with me!"

_____

_____

_____

_____

Exercise 1.5 Andy was in third grade and today was the day that Andy's class got to choose their very own special instruments that they wanted to learn for the rest of their school year. Ever since Andy knew that this day would come he was set on learning the violin because that's what his grandmother used to play when she was his age. Then he took the bow that was carefully placed inside the case and then he held the violin like his grandmother had shown him, he placed his chin on the black color thing which was called the chinrest.

_____

_____

_____

_____

_____

_____
_____
_____
_____
_____
_____

Exercise 1.6 After finishing a quick bowl of cereal …

_____
_____
_____
_____

Exercise 1.7 The second I closed my eyes I was in a deep sleep that I thought no one could bring me out of. After about 2 or 3 minutes of being asleep I began to dream.

_____
_____
_____
_____

2. Alliteration:

Using the same letter to begin two or more words (or even every word) in a phrase or sentence. Alliteration adds a rhythmic effect to the phrase or sentence.

Examples:

2.1 There were boys banging bats against broken boards.

2.2 From her bedroom came the sound of wonderful, wild, wacky laughter.

2.3 Tom threw tomatoes at the third graders teasing him.

Exercise 2.1 Create two sentences that each contain an example of alliteration.

_____
_____
_____
_____
_____
_____
_____
_____
_____

3. Foreshadowing

When an author places a hint in his story that something will happen in the story later on, before it actually happens, this is foreshadowing. Authors use this technique to tease the reader, to arouse the reader's curiosity and motivate the reader to keep reading to see what happens.

Examples (the foreshadowing is shown in bold text):

3.1. After John and Sam played John's new video game for the millionth time, it was time for Sam to go home. They promised to get together the next day. **But how could John know that he would never see Sam again?**

3.2. Mary's career as a child actress seemed to be going nowhere. Six auditions in two weeks…but no callbacks. What she didn't know was that Steven Spielberg, the famous movie director, had seen a clip of the auditions. **Soon her life would change.**

Comment: after this foreshadowing hint, the story continues on; Mary sat home, alone in her room, discouraged…wondering what she was doing wrong. How could she find someone to help her? Eventually the author reveals how her life changed.

Exercise 3.1 Create two paragraphs that each contain an example of Foreshadowing.

_____

_____

_____

_____

_____

_____

4. Simile

A comparison that shows how two things, living or nonliving, that are not alike in most ways are alike in the way described in the simile. The words "like" or "as" are always used in a simile.

Examples:

1.1. He eats like a pig. *Comment: comparing the way a person eats with how a pig eats.*

1.2. Muhammad Ali, the famous heavyweight boxer, used these similes to compare his boxing style to two insects: "Float like a butterfly, sting like a bee".

Comment: who would have thought to compare a heavyweight boxer's boxing style to a butterfly and a bee? That is really an original comparison.

Creating a simile is an opportunity to use your imagination to create a comparison that is really original. Can you think up a comparison that is creative? Try it.

Exercise 4.1 Create two phrases that each contain an example of a Simile.

_____

_____

_____

_____

5. Metaphor

Like a simile, a metaphor describes something that two very different things have in common, but unlike a simile, the words "like" or "as" are never used. A metaphor is especially effective if the author compares two things that the reader never thought had similarities.

Examples:

1.1. Sea gulls gliding, sweeping, turning in a ballet of nature. ***Comment: usually you think of dancers in a ballet, not sea gulls.***

1.2. The pasture was a carpet of green. ***Comment: usually you think of a pasture as a field of grass, not as a carpet.***

Exercise 5.1 Create two sentences that each contain an example of a Metaphor.

_____

_____

_____

_____

_____

_____

_____

_____

6. Onomatopoeia

Words that when spoken (out loud or in your mind) make a sound like the sound they describe.

Examples:

1.1. He slurped (or slurrrrped) his soup.

1.2. He heard the loud VRRROOM, VRRROOM of a motorcycle revving up.

1.3. The washing machine SWISH-SWISHED, SWISH SWISHED.

1.4. The rain went rat-a-tat-tat, rat-a-tat-tat on the windowpane.

1.5. Woof woof!! Meow meow!

Exercise 6.1 Create two phrases that each contain an example of Onomatopoeia.

_____

_____

_____

_____

_____

_____

7. Repeating words, phrases and sentences

Repeating the same word, phrase or sentence is a technique authors use to emphasize a thought or idea to a reader - that is, to make it clear to the reader that the thought or idea is important, even though the repetition is not necessary for the sentence or phrase or paragraph to make sense. Repetition is also used to bundle together into one theme several descriptive words or phrases or sentences.

Examples:

1.1. Is there anything so thrilling, so exciting, so cool as a ride on a modern roller coaster?

1.2. It was as gross, as disgusting, as ugly as an animal could be.

1.3. You should hear this CD. You should hear them sing. Music to make you move, music to make you sing along, music to make you smile, music to make you forget sad things.

1.4. My family loves hugs.

My mom hugs me when she wakes me up in the morning for school.

My dad hugs me when he comes home from work.

My sister hugs me when she comes home from college to visit.

And I hug them for no reason.

1.5. My father was a great basketball player years ago.

Even now, he is still good.

He knows how to dribble.

He knows how to head fake then drive.

He knows how to make a turnaround jump shot.

He knows how to slam dunk.

He knows how to win our one-on one games, and

He knows that he must win while he can, because I get better and better.

1.6. It started with a small group in one town, then it spread throughout the county, then it spread throughout the state, and then it spread to two adjoining states, at which point the national news media picked up on it

Exercise 7.1 Create two paragraphs that each contain an example of repeating words, phrases and sentences

_____
_____
_____
_____
_____
_____
_____
_____
_____

8. Using the same sentence structure in a group of sentences

This technique can be used: to add a flow, a rhythm to events in the story; to cover several events or time periods with just a few words (because the author needs to move the story along to reveal events more important to him or her than the events he or she skims over); or to slow the reader down so that the reader will have time to realize that events are taking place over a long time period, even though the sentence(s) that describe these events are short.

Examples:

1.1. They got into the car, and drove and ate and took naps, and drove and ate and took naps, and drove some more and ate some more and took naps some more, until they saw the city lights in the distance, and they knew they were almost home.

1.2. And they won their last five games, and then the local championship and then the Group II state title and then they all went to the Athletic Awards dinner and relaxed and ate and told basketball stories about each other and laughed the evening away.

Exercise 8.1 Create two paragraphs that each contain an example of a repeating sentence structure.

_____
_____
_____
_____
_____
_____
_____
_____
_____

9. Using "and" in a different way

Instead of using commas, this technique repeats the word "and" to emphasize (to focus the reader on) words, phrases and sentences and separate them from other related words, phrases and sentences, yet tie them all together in a related bundle. Using "and" instead of commas also slows the reader down and forces the reader to realize that although the author is trying to cover a long time period or many events in a few short words or phrases or sentences, the author wants the reader to be aware of each of these events introduced by each "and", and not skim over them and miss their details. This technique is also included in the examples given in 8 above.

Exercise 9.1 Create two sentences showing the use of "and" instead of commas.

_____

_____

_____

_____

_____

_____

_____

_____

10. Sentence fragments

Phrases that are not complete sentences. Sentence fragments can say a lot in a few words, because they eliminate verbs and consonants and any words that are not necessary for the reader to understand the meaning of the phrase.

Examples:

1.1. My friend Tom. Dirty face. Mussed up hair. Torn pants.
Comment: this is more dramatic than if full sentences were used, such as "See my friend Tom. Notice his dirty face and his mussed up hair and his torn pants.

1.2. Sara! Sara! Stop! Stop now! No! No! Don't go there!
Comment: the sentence fragments can be read faster by the reader than full sentences, which adds to the urgency of the situation that the author wants to create in the reader's mind.

Exercise 10.1 Create two phrases that are sentence fragments.

_____

_____

_____

_____

11. Runaway or Run-on Sentence

A runaway sentence is a sentence that is very long. When a teacher/parent sees such a sentence, he or she may tell the author to break up this sentence into several shorter sentences. But there are instances when a runaway sentence is an excellent technique for an author to tell about a very exciting or emotional event or series of events, such as scoring a goal in a soccer game, or scoring the winning basket in basketball, or when a fast moving tragedy or disaster occurs in which an author needs to give the reader a lot of detail about someone or something and wants to pull the reader along all the way through until the end of the event. Breaking such a sentence into several smaller sentences risks losing the reader's focus and emotions. A runaway sentence may be its own paragraph.

Example:

I roared up the half pipe on my skateboard, higher than ever before, within inches of the top, but as I did my jump turn, I lost my balance and fell backward, off the end of the ramp and toward the ground. The rest was a blur. Voices loud and anxious, someone asking me "Can you hear me? Can you hear me?," Then blackness, the sound of a siren, the blur of red flashing lights, hands sliding me gently on to a stretcher, then blackness, then the feelings of swaying and bumping inside a speeding ambulance, more questions, conversations, hands gently on my forehead, someone taking my pulse.

Comment: the author wants to grab your attention and hold it until he or she finishes the action.

Exercise 11.1 Create two runaway sentences.

_____

_____

_____

_____

_____

_____

_____

12. Other Techniques

1.1. Intentional Misspelling: misspelling words on purpose to achieve a certain purpose.

Examples: Awakening in the warm sunlight, the cat streeeeeetched and yawwwwwwned. They went sliiiiiiding down the hill. Mom, dad, puleeease!!

1.2 Eliminating spaces between words on purpose: This technique is used to make a phrase or sentence appear more urgent to a reader; it communicates rapid action or urgent conversation.

Examples: Tumbling headoverheels, headoverheels, or Getdownherenow!!

Exercise 12.1 Create two phrases that each contain an example of an intentionally misspelled word. The misspelled words must be words that create a more interesting mental picture (ex. yawwwwning or streeeeetching) than the correctly spelled words (ex. yawning or stretching).

_____
_____
_____
_____
_____
_____

Exercise 12.2 Create two phrases that each contain several words jammed together (no spaces between) to create a sense of urgency.

_____
_____
_____
_____
_____
_____

EXERCISE 13:

Write several paragraphs and/or short stories that include one or more of the techniques in paragraphs 2 through 12 above. The text that you write must be original. You must include at least one example of each technique in each paragraph or short story.

_____
_____
_____
_____
_____
_____
_____
_____
_____
_____
_____
_____
_____
_____
_____

The CCSSI standards that apply to the preceding paragraphs 2 through 12 are CCSSI: L.6.5,7.3, 7.5 and 8.5.

III. Identifying Illogical or Incomplete Content, Inconsistent Voice (active or passive) and Verb Tense (present and past) and Incorrect Grammar

The author has primary responsibility to make sure that the content of his/her story is: logical and realistic; complete (no details of events, actions or feelings accidentally left incomplete); consistent in the voice and verb tense used; and grammatically correct.

Otherwise, the reader will lose confidence or lose interest in the author and in his story, and may not continue reading the story. An author should want to gain the confidence of every reader, especially if the story is nonfiction and/or the author is trying to persuade the reader to accept his opinion or point of view on a topic.

In this chapter, redundant or unnecessary text is shown with a strikethrough line through it; text that is being added is enclosed in brackets [ ]; and *comments are shown in italic type.* The answers to Exercises 1.1 to 1.5 are in Chapter XIII. ANSWERS.

Here are examples of illogical content (also called "faulty logic" or "not logical content").

EXERCISES:

Can you explain what is illogical about each story line?

Exercise 1.1 In the American West in the 1800's, army soldiers set up camp as night fell. They were at war with the Indian tribes who lived there. The commanding officer always sent out lookouts to nearby hilltops to watch all night for Indians massing for an attack.

This night, a lookout spotted hundreds of Indians moving toward the soldiers' encampment. The lookout immediately sent a text message from his handheld phone to his commander, warning of an impending Indian attack. The commander was able to awaken his troops and get them into position so they were successful in repelling the Indian attack.

_____

_____

_____

Exercise 1.2 In the summer of 2010, my family and I travelled to New York City to see the sights. We went to Rockefeller Center to see the skating rink, to the Museum of Modern Art, and boarded a Gray Line boat for a cruise around Manhattan. The view from the boat was spectacular: we saw the Empire State Building, Statue of Liberty, Golden Gate Bridge and planes taking off and landing at Newark Liberty Airport.

_____
_____
_____
_____
_____
_____
_____
_____

Exercise 1.3 My grandmother is 80 years old. She grew up on a farm in the Midwest. When she was your age, in 1941, she went to sleep one night, but was awakened by loud claps of thunder and flashes of lightning. She looked out her window and saw flames shooting out the barn door.
Frantic, she switched on the light and went screaming into her parent's room. Her mother grabbed the phone and pressed the 9-1-1 buttons. The 9-1-1 operator answered and called the fire department. Most of the barn was saved.

_____
_____
_____
_____
_____
_____

Exercise 1.4 My grandmother told me another story, also from 1941. From her bedroom window in the farm house, she could see a long distance across the fields. One day during the summer, their phone rang, and when her mother picked up the receiver, a frantic neighbor told her to switch on CNN because they were broadcasting a tornado warning for their town, complete with actual live footage. It was very scary; fortunately the tornado veered off to the south and away from their farm.

_____
_____
_____
_____

Exercise 1.5 Hi. My name is George. This year, 2010, I am a senior in high school. I have a funny story to tell you. Five years ago, when I was in seventh grade, I got a Wii controller with a tennis game diskette for my birthday. One day my mom asked me to let her try it. You won't believe what happened!!

_____

_____

_____

_____

Example: Here is an example of incomplete content, inconsistent verb tense, and redundant phrases: Lyra was going into 4th grade and she wasn't so excited about this move. THUD THUD. The car ~~had gone on over a hump~~, [_went over a speed bump_] and ~~suddenly she~~ woke [_her_] ~~up~~ from a deep sleep.

Incomplete content: The author should explain why Lyra was not excited about the move. Examples of explanations the author could have used are: leaving all her friends and having to make new ones, or going to a new country which would have different customs.
Inconsistent verb tense: "had gone over" is past tense; "woke her" is present tense. To make both tenses agree, change "had gone over" to "went over."
Redundant phrases: Unnecessary words have been marked with strikethrough lines and substitute words enclosed in brackets

Example:
Here are more examples of incomplete content:
1. India is a really interesting place. There are many different religions, cars, etc… There are also many cars that look different than the cars that are in America.
The author should either name some of the different religions and cars or delete those sentences.
2. Jonathan Burke was the son of Thompson and Mary Burke, who owned the biggest toy shop in the world. John was 11 years old and lived with his uncle, Norris Burke, who was the owner of a large farm in California.
The author should explain why Jonathan is not living with his parents, which would have been the normal situation.

Here are examples of incorrect grammar:

1. "Mum, Mum where are all the kids who live here? I don't see anyone riding ~~their~~ bikes.

"anyone" is singular, but "their" is plural. The author should have used the singular form, either "riding his bike" or just "riding bikes."

2. Then her mother turned back to see Lyra's father still sleeping in the car. "Well, am I the only one that didn't sleep in the car?" she said.
"that" refers to a non-human object; "who" refers to a person; the author should have used "who" in this sentence

Here are examples of redundant phrases and inconsistent voices.

3. Redundant phrase and inconsistent voice: But the second I closed my eyes I was in a deep sleep that I thought no one except for my mom and her raging voice could bring me out of. After a few minutes of being asleep the dream started.

Redundant phrase "of being asleep": The author has already said the character is asleep in the preceding sentence.
Inconsistent voice: "After a few minutes of being asleep, the dream started" is passive voice. Up to this point, the author used active voice ("I closed, I thought"), so to be consistent, use "I started to dream" instead of "the dream started."

 CCSSI: W.6.3, 7.3, 8.3.
CCSSI: L.6.1, 7.1, L.8.1

IV. Expressing the Emotions of a Character: Show, Don't Tell!!

The most creative ways for an author to describe the emotions being felt, expressed or acted out by the characters in a story, with or without using pictures, is to describe the physical characteristics, the actions taken, and the thoughts and/or words spoken by these characters as they experience the emotion, in such a way that the reader figures out what the emotion is. This is what we mean by showing emotions.

Showing emotions is much more creative than telling the reader what the emotion is using single words like angry, happy, sad, etc. An author who communicates a character's emotions by showing them to the reader instead of telling them to the reader is forcing the reader to figure out the emotions based on the clues in the detailed descriptions that the author has given.

How does an author show emotions to the reader? Look at the following table for some ideas.

WAYS TO SHOW EMOTIONS	DETAILED DESCRIPTIONS
Facial expressions	**Eyes**: narrow (like slits), glaring, wide open, sparkling. **Eyebrows**: raised and forehead wrinkled, eyebrows scrunched toward each other. **Mouth**: closed with lips pressed tightly together, lips curled, corners of mouth turned down or up, lips slightly parted. **Teeth**: gritted (upper and lower teeth together) **Jaws**: upper and lower jaws and mouth open, jaws (and mouth) tightly closed.
Body language and movements	**Open**: welcoming (arms wide and extended, as if ready for a hug). **Closed**: defensive, not receptive (arms folded across chest, arms at sides with fists clenched). **Movements**: Tight, tense, fast or slow, loose, relaxed.
Vocal sounds (written):	**Loud**: Exclamation point, all capital letters, or descriptive words (loud, loudly, shout, yell, scream). **Soft descriptive words** (soft, softly, whispered, murmured).
Facial skin color	Pale, red, purple, flushed.

Examples:

1. Billy came into the room. He was angry. He was frowning, his bushy eyebrows pointed down and his lips, which always turned up when he smiled, were now turned down, and he was gritting his teeth. **Comment: the author doesn't need to tell the reader Billy is angry. The reader will conclude this by the descriptions of his appearance: frowning, eyebrows and lips pointed down, and teeth gritted.**

2. Mary's teammates could tell that Mary was really sad. Usually neat in her appearance, today she was a mess; her hair was scraggly and hanging down, unbrushed, her eyes were red, and she wasn't the smiling happy person that she usually was when she came to softball practice. **Comment: the author doesn't need to tell the reader she was sad, because that is what the sentences that follow do by describing how Mary looked and acted. The first sentence could be changed to read "Mary's teammates could tell that something was bothering her."**

EXERCISES:

Listed below are several different emotions. Using ideas in the table above and/or your own ideas, describe a situation that causes one or more characters to experience each emotion listed below, and describe the character's behavior, actions and/or words that will allow your readers to figure out what the emotion is. REMEMBER – DO NOT use single word descriptions such as angry, happy, sad etc. in your write-ups.

1. Emotion: ANGER (or ANGRY, MAD, FURIOUS).

2. Emotion: JOYFUL (or HAPPY).

3. Emotion: SAD (or UNHAPPY, MISERABLE).

4. Emotion: JEALOUS (or ENVIOUS).

5. Emotion: ARROGANT (or BOASTFUL, CONDESCENDING (looking down on someone or something, treating them/it as inferior)).

6. Emotion: SCARED (or FRIGHTENED).

 CCSSI: W.6.3, 7.3, 8.3.

V. Using the Personification Technique

Personification: giving a character that is not human the ability to do things that humans can do but that that character cannot normally do. Examples: an animal or a rock speaking English, planning a birthday party, building a tree house, playing cards or a board game. Examples of characters to whom personification has been applied: all of the non-human Disney characters; the gecko that sells GEICO products; the non-human Sesame Street characters; Snoopy the dog in the Peanuts cartoon strip; Garfield the cat in the Garfield cartoon strip.

The Personification technique is used very often in movies, plays, cartoon strips and stories. Why do you think it is such a popular technique for authors? Answer: Human beings are the most intelligent creatures on the planet; they are capable of performing more actions and feeling more emotions than any other creature. Therefore, when an author applies personification to an animal, plant or non-living character in a story, the author is giving that character the same abilities that a human has, and can make that character a more interesting character to the reader.

I AM A SWEET DOGGIE!

EXERCISE:

If you are told to write a story about your pet, or if you choose this topic on your own, chances are that you will write the story from your point of view – that is, you will be the story teller. Try something different – write the story as if the pet were telling it (because the pet will be telling the story in English, it means that you, the author, will be using the Personification technique from Chapter V)

_____

_____

_____

_____

_____

_____

_____

_____

_____

_____

_____

_____

_____

_____

_____

_____

_____

_____

_____

_____

_____

_____

_____

_____

_____

_____

_____

_____

_____

_____

_____

_____

_____

_____

_____

_____

_____

_____

_____

_____

_____

_____

_____

_____

 CCSSI: L.6.5, 7.5,8.5

VI. Using the Flashback and Story Within A Story Techniques

Flashback: A flashback happens when the author starts a story in one time period, and part way through the story, changes the time to an earlier period. Because the story moves back in time, the technique is referred to as a flashback. An author has to make it clear to the reader that the story is flashing back, otherwise, the reader may become confused (or, the author may intentionally confuse the reader by not making it clear that a flashback is occurring). To alert the reader that a flashback is or will be occurring, an author uses a "trigger" word or phrase or sentence or paragraph. An example of a trigger sentence is given in the Seabiscuit example below.

Example: A few years ago, an author wrote the novel "Seabiscuit," a true story about a racehorse named Seabiscuit and its jockey. It was written in chronological order; that is, all the events followed one another over time, climaxing with the famous race between Seabiscuit and a champion racehorse named War Admiral. However, the author could have used the flashback technique by beginning the story with the famous race between Seabiscuit and War Admiral, then flashed back to tough times when Seabiscuit and its jockey were both younger and just starting out. To alert the reader to the flashback, the author could end his description of the events surrounding the famous race by using the trigger sentence "But it was not always like this."

Example: Frame story: a college student returns home during a holiday break and one afternoon, while sitting in his bedroom, begins looking through a carton of books in his closet. Trigger sentence #1 (the flashback): Suddenly he sees his high school yearbook, and begins leafing through the pages.
Example: Inner story: As he looks at each page, he remembers events that happened to him and his friends (and these memories become the inner story).
Trigger sentence #2 (return to the frame story): Suddenly the phone rings. It is his hometown friend Tom, also home from college. He puts the yearbook away, puts on his jacket and leaves to meet Tom downtown.

When the author finishes telling about the events that take place in the flashback, the author may choose to end the story or to continue the story by returning to the original time period. The story plot in both the original and flashback time periods must be related; otherwise, the author will have written two independent stories instead of one story with a flashback. Incidentally, the opposite of a flashback is a flash forward, where the story jumps into the future.

Story Within a Story: The story within a story technique can be the same as the flashback or flash forward techniques. Inside one story (*call it the frame story, like a picture frame*) is another story (*call it the inner story, like a picture in a frame*). Like a flashback, the frame and inner stories must be connected by a trigger word, phrase or sentence, otherwise they would be two disconnected, individual stories, not a story within a story. The purpose of the trigger is to move the reader from the frame story to the inner story (*and maybe back to the frame story*). Whereas a flashback or flash forward always use two different time periods, a frame story and an inner story can take place in the same time period, with the inner story interrupting the frame story, or in two different time periods. Either story can be a real event or a dream.

Example: **Frame story:** Shelley is all excited because tomorrow is her birthday and her parents are taking her to the pet store to buy her a puppy. Her mind is full of pictures of she and the puppy doing things together. Trigger sentence: As she does her homework, she begins to feel very tired, falls asleep and begins to dream. Example: Inner story: In her dream, she meets her new puppy, a very unusual puppy who can speak English. They talk about (*the story continues*). Trigger sentence: Shelley is awakened by the buzz of her alarm clock. Return to Frame story: She quickly dresses and rushes downstairs to eat breakfast so she can go and get the puppy. **Comment: Note that in this story, there is no flashback or flash forward. It is told in chronological order; it is always moving forward.**

EXERCISES:

1. Write a story with a flashback in it. Be sure to use a trigger word, phrase, sentence or paragraph.

_____

_____

_____

_____

_____

_____

_____

_____

_____

_____

_____

_____

_____

_____

_____

2. Write a story with a flash forward in it. Be sure to use a trigger word, phrase, sentence or paragraph.

3. Write a story and write another story inside of it. Be sure to use a trigger.

_____

_____

_____

_____

_____

_____

_____

_____

_____

_____

_____

_____

_____

_____

_____

_____

_____

_____

_____

_____

_____

_____

_____

_____

_____

_____

_____

_____

_____

_____

_____

_____

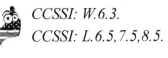

CCSSI: W.6.3.
CCSSI: L.6.5, 7.5, 8.5.

VII. Using the Circular Text Technique

Circular Text is when an author repeats the same (or very similar) words or sentences to begin and end the story. This repetition tells the reader that these words and sentences describe the most important lessons or events or feelings in the story that the author wants the reader to remember.

Example: Let's say that a story begins with these words: "My dog Sam makes me so happy." The author goes on to explain how Sam makes him happy. At the end, Sam grows old and dies. The last sentence says: I will miss my dog Sam; he made me so happy.

Comment: the author stated his main point in the first sentence, which was that his dog Sam makes him happy. But then after telling how Sam made him happy, the author wanted to remind the reader about the main idea, which was that Sam made the author happy, so he repeats the idea in the last sentence..

T.V. and My Family

The TV in our house is very important to me and my family

Comment: As an example of the Circular Text technique, the thought expressed in the first sentence above will be repeated at the end. Also, the author will back up his statement that the TV is important by giving examples in the story. This story is an example of narrative writing.

The TV is used and loved by everyone in my family.

As soon as I come home from school I see my mom watching the TV. She has several favorite daytime TV programs, and she gets so interested in them that when I ask for some food, she tells me to get it myself. Eventually I start watching her shows with her, and once I sit down I almost never get up until the last show ends. She normally watches crime shows, and trying to guess the perpetrator is really entertaining. My father loves to mock these shows, which gets my mother all worked up. If she is really tired after cleaning the house or doing some other hard work, just a half hour of TV takes her mind off of everything and renews her energy.

My father likes to watch TV during and after dinner. He likes watching shows produced in English, especially comedies. However, he also likes one mystery show called White Collar, which is all about cons in the USA stealing very valuable things. All four of us enjoy that show.

My brother is a TV maniac! Whenever I see him on weekends he is glued to the TV. My mom has to drag him to the table during meal times. He loves to watch cartoons and loathes anything with real people except for Harry Potter. Unlike the rest of the family, my brother gets really hyper when he watches TV; he is completely uncontrollable and starts jumping up and down or fighting just like the characters on TV.

Comment: In the preceding sentence, a semicolon is used to separate two sentences that are very closely related, instead of splitting them into separate sentences.

   I love TV more than anyone in my family because it relaxes me and when I am angry, it calms me down. But I never get as much time to watch it as the rest of the family does, because I always have a lot of homework or other things that I need to get done. Whenever I get a day off from my hectic schedule I watch as much TV as possible, but even then my parents restrict me from watching it too much. They always say "too little is bad and too much is also bad"

   Everyone in my family loves TV, and we all have our reasons. TV is not only very important to me, but it is also very important to my family.

Comment: The author has been successful in explaining why his family loves TV, which back up his statements in the first and last sentences of the story.

EXERCISE:

Write a story in which you use the circular text technique.

_____

_____

_____

_____

_____

_____

_____

_____

_____

_____

_____

_____

_____

_____

_____

_____

_____

_____

_____

_____

_____

_____

_____

_____

CCSSI: L.6.5, 7.5,8.5.

VIII. Using the Five Senses

Human beings (and other characters that an author has personified with human capabilities) have five senses: sight, hearing, touch, smell and taste.

Any or all of these senses can influence the actions a character takes and the thoughts a character thinks, in the following ways:

• by influencing what a character does (runs away, runs toward, hugs, punches, shoots, stands silently);

• by influencing what a character says and how he or she says it (encouraging, discouraging, compassionate, hateful, said loudly, said softly, said quickly, said slowly);

• by influencing what a character thinks (the emotions and possible reactions that run through the character's mind, from extreme panic to extreme joy).

Example: Here is an example of how the five senses can be used in a story.

<u>The Restaurant</u>

Comment: This is narrative writing whose purpose it is to entertain. It can also be considered expository writing, because the reader can learn what a restaurant consultant looks for when doing his job.

I am a restaurant consultant who has been hired by a new owner to visit his restaurant and advise him on how he can attract more customers to the restaurant and reverse a recent decline in its profits. This is what took place during that visit.

I arrived at the restaurant, went inside to meet the owner, and said: "You have a great location here, on this major highway just outside of town. Let me start my observations by walking around the outside with you!" After a short time looking at the outside, I said: "An important reason why people choose to come to a restaurant, especially travelers who are just passing through and are not familiar with the area, is the way it looks on the outside. Customers notice whether the restaurant's sign is attractively lettered and in good condition, and whether the exterior walls of the restaurant are well maintained. In your case, the paint on the sign is peeling and there is a green stain in one corner. Also, the paint on the exterior walls is peeling. They also look for a neat and clean parking area; yours needs a good cleanup…look at the trash on the ground, and why are your garbage cans visible from the parking lot? And what is it that smells so bad? I guess it is the odor from the garbage cans. Customers are going to be turned off by that, too. These are some reasons why this restaurant is not making enough money. Now let's take a look inside."

We began in the dining room. "Look at your carpeting – it has worn through in several places. The wallpaper is peeling, and the lighting is too dim. The place looks like an old rundown pub that has seen better times, not like a family-friendly restaurant. Your chairs and tables are worn, outdated and stained. Let's go into the kitchen" I said. We walked into the kitchen where cooks were preparing the lunch service. I asked a waiter for a menu; he handed me a single sheet of paper that listed the menu items. I was astonished; no menu cover with plastic sheets to protect the menu. "This menu is not presented in an appealing manner," I said.

I examined the menu items; the selection was good, and consisted of the kinds of items that would appeal to the average customer. There was roast beef, several kinds of salads, Italian pizza with a choice of toppings, onion rings, chicken wings and so much more. The smells of the food in the kitchen were appealing also. The kitchen was very clean and well maintained except that the wallpaper was peeling. Then I wondered, who puts wallpaper in a kitchen? We walked out of the kitchen and sat at a table. I said "There are some appealing things about your menu and your kitchen; however, you are going to have to make some changes in the kitchen."

"Before I finish my list of suggestions for improvements, I would like to sample some of the food from your menu." I said. "Of course. Tell me which items you would like to try," the owner said. After a short time the waiters brought the food. The first thing that I did was look at how the food was presented, and how large the portion sizes were. "The presentations are very basic and plain – not creative. And while some portions are adequate, others are too small for the prices charged." I said. Next, I smelled the food, then tested its consistency with a knife, fork, spoon or my fingers, and finally I tasted the food. Each food item smelled good, and when I poked at it with a utensil, it had the right feel – the tenderness or creaminess or color that reflected how much the item had been cooked (rare, medium rare, etc.) Then came the taste tests. Most of the food tasted very good, except for the soup and some of the desserts. I mentioned all of these observations to the owner.

I also noticed something else, as I sat at my table: the restaurant was noisy with conversation, and they had a radio tuned to the local talk and music station. It was distracting.

Now it was time to document my findings. I took out my checklist and wrote:
 1) Repaint the outside walls
2) Clean, repaint and re-letter the sign
3) Replace the inside lighting with brighter and more attractive lights
4) Get new and more comfortable cushioned chairs and new tables
5) Replace wallpaper in dining area and remove it from the kitchen
6) Instead of using canned or packaged, manufactured products, use fresh, homemade ingredients in your soups and either make your desserts yourself or import them from your local bakery

7) Get professionally designed and printed menus.

8) Ideally, you should add noise deadening materials such as acoustic ceiling tiles, curtains and carpets,

But I realize you may not be able to afford these things now. A change you can make now is to purchase a CD player and hook it up to the speaker system, to play quiet, soothing music for your customers. They looked at the list and asked, "How much do you think all of this will cost?"

"Well" I replied "I need a little time to estimate these costs, but a rough estimate is several thousand dollars." They just nodded.

As I drove back to my hotel, I thought "This is going to be a great restaurant when I am through with it."

EXERCISE:

On a separate piece of paper, make 5 columns. Label the columns sight, hearing, touch, smell and taste. Read the story "The Restaurant" above and place a hash mark (a hash mark is a vertical line |) for each example where the consultant used one of his five senses. The answers are presented in Chapter XIII. Answers.

 CCSSI: W.6.3, 7.3, 8.3

IX. Using the Persuasion Technique

Whenever the content of the "Eat More Ketchup" write-up meets one of the CCSSI requirements for a persuasive argument, the editor has inserted the following text: [CCSSI: (text of the requirement appears here)].

Writing errors in the content will be identified with a comment in the format *[Comment: (text of the comment)]*; unnecessary text or text for which a better word choice is made in brackets, will be identified with a strike through line; text added will be enclosed in brackets *[ ]*.

Eat More Ketchup! It Tastes Good and It's Healthy

Comment: This is persuasive writing whose purpose it is to persuade the reader to agree with the author's viewpoint. The author's viewpoint is expressed well in the title.

In America, ketchup is a very popular complement to many foods. People like its flavor.

When they are eating ketchup, what do they notice in its taste? Tomatoes, some spices and maybe some artificial ~~tastes~~ [flavors]. But no one can taste lycopene, an ingredient in the tomatoes in ketchup, that is a strong anti-oxidant and therefore very important for the health of our bodies. *[CCSSI: Introduce claims]*. Why is lycopene important to our ~~body~~ [bodies]? *[Comment: "bodies" was used in the prior sentence, and to be consistent, should continue to be used in this write-up.]*

[CCSSI Introduce reasons that support the claim(s)]. In our ~~body~~ *[bodies]* there ~~is~~ *[are]* some things called ~~a~~ free radicals. Free radicals are ~~free~~ *[unpaired]* electrons that are attached to atoms or molecules. These free radicals can oxidize most of the molecules in our ~~body~~*[bodies]. [Comment: The author does not tell us whether this is good or bad for us.]*

However these little devils are [also] known to oxidize the DNA molecules in the cell nucleus. If this happens, ~~then~~ the body has an increased chance of getting cancer and other deadly diseases. ~~So Lycopene in the tomatoes~~ *[Comment: we were already told that it is in the tomatoes]* eats these free radicals and stops them from oxidizing the DNA molecules. *[CCSSI: Support claim(s)(of lycopene's health benefits) with clear reasons and relevant evidence, using credible sources and demonstrating an understanding of the topic or text.]*

~~Some of~~ [If] you ~~may be~~ [are] wondering what "oxidize" means, *[here is an example that will help you understand it]*. The Statue of Liberty in New York is really made of copper. When the French first made it and handed it over to the United States, it was the color of a penny, a nice brown, gold copper color. But over the years, the color has changed to a light green. This happens because the copper molecules mix with the oxygen molecules in the air and they form a new substance called copper oxide. ~~This is what has happened to the Statue of Liberty. The copper in the statue has changed color to a light green due to the mixing of molecules over the years.~~ *[Comment: Redundant - you have already explained this.]* To summarize: the process of mixing oxygen with other substances such as copper is called oxidation.

Believe it or not, there are many antioxidants found in other fruits and vegetables besides tomatoes. For example, carrots, watermelons, papayas and many more. That is why so many nutritionists recommend that you include fruits and vegetables in your daily diet.

Now that I think of it, what would have happened if we had put ketchup all over the Statue of Liberty to prevent it from changing color? That would be something not only to see but also to eat!!!

EXERCISE:

Choose a subject you feel strongly about and write a narrative to try and persuade the readers to agree with your point of view. Make sure your narrative uses all of the requirements for an argument that are presented in the CCSSI standards description shown below

 CCSSI: W.6.1,7.1,8.1.

X. The Role of the Setting in a Story

In Chapter I "Four Ways to Expand a Story Idea into a Story," we defined <u>the setting of a story as the location where an event or a relationship takes place, or the time period in which an event or relationship takes place.</u> A location is usually a place that is tangible, that is, a place you can touch, feel, smell or see, such as a classroom, pasture, stadium, racetrack, mountaintop, ocean, lake, or room in a home, such as the kitchen. A setting and its physical characteristics can play a major role in a story by influencing how the plot, events and characters play out. For example, in a sports story about a championship playoff, the location of the stadium, the weather, the banners and clothing displayed by the crowd, and the presence of marching bands are usually very important. A physical setting can be impacted by a natural event such as an earthquake or a hurricane, which can also influence how a plot and its characters play out.

Besides tangible (touchable) settings, there are settings that are imaginary, such as heaven, or in a character's mind.

Also included in the definition of a setting is the time period in which a story takes place. A time period can be in the past, present, or future and a story may take place in one or more time periods. The time period(s) in which a story takes place can have a major influence on how a plot and its characters play out. To make sure his story is authentic, an author has to be careful to include only those inventions, events, vocabulary and props (example: clothing, video equipment, computers) that existed in the time period in which his story is written.

Sometimes the setting is not important. For example, in a story based on a conversation between two people, the important part of the story may be what is said; where or when the conversation takes place may not matter much.

<u>Hints for a physical setting</u>: Think about natural and manmade things that could appear in the setting. Think about the physical appearance of people, animals, plants or nonliving things in the setting, the sounds or smells in the setting, the presence of light or darkness in the setting.
Example: It was a ~~fine~~ [sunny, warm] August afternoon.
Comment: "fine" is too vague; describe it as sunny and warm.

<u>Hints for a time period setting</u>: Think about whether the presence and appearance of characters or

things in the setting are logical for that time period. Example: If the story takes place in the 1960's, some nonconforming teenagers had long hair and peace symbols on their clothes. Also, in 1964, the Ford Mustang and the Beatles were introduced. The first landing on the moon by U.S. astronauts was made during the Apollo 11 flight in 1969. Stories that take place now could refer to cell phones and iPods and laptop readers and Facebook and Twitter.

Remember: The author is responsible for making sure that the clothing, vocabulary, actors and performers and movies and plays, locations and events actually had been invented or were in use during the time period of the story, unless the story is fantasy fiction.

EXERCISES:

Read each story and do the assignment that follows each story.

<u>Story #1: An Abandoned House</u>

Jimmy and his family had just moved into the neighborhood. Jimmy met Joey and Billy, his neighbors, and they became good friends.One day they decided to walk to the amusement arcade to play some games. Just when the sun was setting, they started to walk home, and this time they took a shortcut through some woods. Suddenly Jimmy noticed a house in the woods. "Who lives there?" he asked. "No one" said Billy. "Can we go inside and look around?" Jimmy asked. "I –I don't want to" said Billy. "Me either" said Joey.

"Aw, c'mon, it's only an empty house." said Jimmy. "Maybe it is and maybe it isn't. I don't want to find out." said Billy. "I'm going in." said Jimmy, "and if you don't come with me, I'm telling everyone in our class that you are both chicken."

Assignment: Describe what a scary house setting would look like from the outside. Describe what the boys saw, heard, felt, smelled etc. when they went inside the house; make the description very scary.

Story #2. Changing the Amusement Park

The committee in charge of planning the amusements on the town's boardwalk has a problem: the rides, game booths and games arcade are old and out of date. Colors are fading, paint is peeling, no new games have been purchased recently and attendance keeps dropping. Last summer, committee members came to the boardwalk and stopped a lot of kids to ask them if they were visiting the amusement area, and if not, why not. Many said they were not; the two main reasons: "We have seen and done everything that is there;" "It looks old and it is boring."

After hearing this, the committee in charge formed another committee to figure out what to do to make the amusements more interesting. You are on that committee.

Assignment: Create and describe changes to the present amusement park setting that you think would attract you and your friends to the amusement rides, booths and arcade on the town's boardwalk.

CCSSI: W.6.3.

XI. Presenting and Supporting Theories (Claims)

The following essay on global warming is an example of expository writing. Its purpose is to explain the concept of global warming and present claims and evidence to support two viewpoints about global warming. If the author draws a conclusion about global warming and recommends actions that the reader should take, then this write-up also qualifies as persuasive writing.

<u>Global Warming</u>

Claims: Since the start of civilization, humans have been aware of the effects of temperature on them when they are on land and at sea. For many years, scientists have been studying the effects of temperature on living organisms on planet Earth. *Claim and Conclusion*: In the last few years, global warming has been recognized as a very important environmental phenomenon that can have dramatic and devastating effects on the environment of planet Earth.

Definition: What is global warming? Global warming is an increase in the earth's atmospheric and oceanic temperatures … (occurring) due to an increase in the greenhouse effect, and resulting especially from pollution.[12] Stated another way: the recent increase in the world's temperature that is believed to be caused by the increase of certain gases (such as carbon dioxide) in the atmosphere.

Definition: The greenhouse effect is the warming of the Earth's atmosphere that is caused by air pollution. The greenhouse effect occurs when warmth from the sun is trapped in the Earth's atmosphere by a layer of gases (such as carbon dioxide) and water vapor.

Claim: Global warming is currently the subject of intense investigation and discussion among scientists, teachers, reporters and the general human population. *Preview of what will follow*: This document will present some theories (claims) about global warming, reasons that support these theories and evidence that supports these theories.

Claim: There are two primary theories (sometimes called claims) about the causes of global warming and the greenhouse effect. One theory (we'll call it Theory #1) believes that human activities are the principal causes of global warming and the greenhouse effect. Another theory (we'll call it Theory #2) believes that global warming is not just a recent phenomenon, but is a natural phenomenon that has been occurring for thousands of years as part of a cycle of warming and cooling of the earth's atmosphere, and that human activity is only a minor contributor.

Author's Notes:

1. Because Theory #2 is a contradiction of Theory #1, it is sometimes called a counterclaim, an alternate claim, or an opposing claim. If Theory #2 agreed with or added to Theory #1, it could be called a supporting claim or complementary claim.

2. The following essay is not meant to be a comprehensive treatment of the subject of global warming; it has been written only to show an example of an essay that meets the writing standards mentioned above.

3. The four paragraphs above are an introduction to the Global Warming document. They meet these requirements from standard W.7.1: Introduce claim(s), acknowledge alternate or opposing claims. They also meet these requirements from W.7.2: Introduce a topic clearly, previewing what is to follow; organize ideas, concepts, and information, using strategies such as definition, and cause/effect... AND Use precise language and domain-specific vocabulary to inform about or explain the topic.

THEORY #1: Human activities are the principal causes of global warming and the greenhouse effect.
Is It Happening?

Claim: Yes. Earth is already showing many signs of worldwide climate change.

Evidence:
• Average temperatures have climbed 1.4 degrees Fahrenheit (0.8 degree Celsius) around the world since 1880, much of this in recent decades, according to NASA's Goddard Institute for Space Studies.

• Arctic ice is rapidly disappearing, and the region may have its first completely ice-free summer by 2040 or earlier. Polar bears and indigenous cultures are already suffering from the sea-ice loss.

• Glaciers and mountain snows are rapidly melting—for example, Montana's Glacier National Park now has only 27 glaciers, versus 150 in 1910. In the Northern Hemisphere, thaws also come a week earlier in spring and freezes begin a week later.
• An upsurge in the amount of extreme weather events, such as wildfires, heat waves, and strong tropical storms, is also attributed in part to climate change by some experts.

Claim and Conclusion: An IPCC (United Nations' Intergovernmental Panel on Climate Change) report, based on the work of some 2,500 scientists in more than 130 countries, concluded that humans have caused all or most of the current planetary warming. Human-caused global warming is often called anthropogenic climate change. Industrialization, deforestation, and pollution have greatly increased atmospheric concentrations of water vapor, carbon dioxide, methane, and nitrous oxide, all greenhouse gases that help trap heat near Earth's surface.

Humans are pouring carbon dioxide into the atmosphere much faster than plants and oceans can absorb it.

Author's Note: "Is It Happening" meets these requirements from standard W.7.1: Support claim(s) with logical reasoning and relevant evidence, using accurate, credible sources and demonstrating an understanding of the topic or text, AND Use words, phrases, and clauses to create cohesion and clarify the relationships among claim(s), reasons, and evidence, AND Provide a concluding statement or section that follows from and supports the information or explanation presented.
It also meets these requirements from standard W.7.2: Develop the topic with relevant facts, definitions, concrete details, quotations, or other information and examples, AND Use precise language and domain-specific vocabulary to inform about or explain the topic, AND Provide a concluding statement or section that follows from and supports the information or explanation presented.

What's Going to Happen?

Claims and Conclusions: A follow-up report by the IPCC released in April 2007 warned that global warming could lead to large-scale food and water shortages and have catastrophic effects on wildlife
• Sea level could rise between 7 and 23 inches (18 to 59 centimeters) by century's end, the IPCC's February 2007 report projects. Rises of just 4 inches (10 centimeters) could flood many South Seas islands and swamp large parts of Southeast Asia.

• Some hundred million people live within 3 feet (1 meter) of mean sea level, and much of the world's population is concentrated in vulnerable coastal cities. In the U.S., Louisiana and Florida are especially at risk.

• Glaciers around the world could melt, causing sea levels to rise while creating water shortages in regions dependent on runoff for fresh water.
• Strong hurricanes, droughts, heat waves, wildfires, and other natural disasters may become commonplace in many parts of the world. The growth of deserts may also cause food shortages in many places.
• More than a million species face extinction from disappearing habitat, changing ecosystems, and acidifying oceans.
• The ocean's circulation system, known as the ocean conveyor belt, could be permanently altered, causing a mini-ice age in Western Europe and other rapid changes.
• At some point in the future, warming could become uncontrollable by creating a so-called positive feedback effect. Rising temperatures could release additional greenhouse gases by unlocking methane in permafrost and undersea deposits, freeing carbon trapped in sea ice, and causing increased evaporation of water.

Author's Note: "What's Going to Happen?" meets these requirements from standard W.7.2: Introduce a topic clearly ...; organize ideas, concepts, and information, using strategies such as ...cause/ effect...AND from standards W.7.1 and W.7.2: Provide a concluding statement or section that follows from and supports the argument presented[13] Ibid.

THEORY #2: Global warming is not just a recent event, but is a natural phenomenon that has been occurring for thousands of years as part of a cycle of warming and cooling of the earth's atmosphere, and that human activity is only a minor contributor.

31,000 scientists say "no convincing evidence" [13]
Claim and Evidence: 31,000 scientists reject global warming and say "no convincing evidence" that humans can or will cause global warming. This claim originates from the <u>Oregon Institute of Science and Medicine</u>, which has an online petition that they claim 31,000 scientists have signed.

Author's Note: The above paragraph is a claim. The preceding paragraph meets this requirement from standard W.7.1: Support claim(s) with logical reasoning and relevant evidence, using accurate, credible sources and demonstrating an understanding of the topic or text.

Claim and Evidence: But polls show that of scientists working in the field of climate science, and publishing papers on the topic: 97% of the climate scientists surveyed believe "global average temperatures have increased" during the past century; and 97% think human activity is a significant contributing factor in changing mean global temperatures. Do '31,000 scientists say global warming is not real'? Maybe. But how important a number is that? They are not talking about only climate scientists. You could have a PhD in anthropology or religion, but what expertise does one have in climatology? That is the more important question.

Author's Note: The preceding paragraph is a counterclaim to the claim in the first paragraph, and challenges whether the claim made in that paragraph meets the criteria of relevant evidence.
That paragraph also meets this requirement from standard W.7.2: Introduce a topic clearly...; organize ideas, concepts, and information, using strategies such as ...comparison/contrast....
Author's Note: Both of the preceding paragraphs meet this requirement from standard W.7.1: Support claim(s) with logical reasoning and relevant evidence, using accurate, credible sources and demonstrating an understanding of the topic or text.

Claim, Evidence and Conclusion: Natural Cycles: Some experts point out that natural cycles in Earth's orbit can alter the planet's exposure to sunlight, which may explain the current trend. Earth has indeed experienced warming and cooling cycles roughly every hundred thousand years due to these orbital shifts, but such changes have occurred over the span of several centuries. ***Author's Note: The next sentence is a rebuttal from a believer in Theory #1. Evidence:*** Today's changes have taken place

over the past hundred years or less[13]

Author's Note: The preceding paragraph meets this requirement from standard W.7.1: Support claim(s) with logical reasoning and relevant evidence....

What is Climategate? [14]

Evidence: In late November 2009, hackers unearthed hundreds of emails at the U.K.'s University of East Anglia that exposed private conversations among top-level British and U.S. climate scientists discussing whether certain data should be released to the public. The email exchanges also refer to statistical tricks used to illustrate climate change trends, and call climate skeptics idiots, according to the New York Times.

Claims: Climate change skeptics have heralded the emails as an attempt to fool the public, according to the Times. [14] Ibid.

Conclusion

Based on the facts and opinions in this document, I (the author) conclude that ....

Author's Notes: Assume the author expressed his conclusions about this topic.
If the author recommended action by the reader to support the author's conclusions, then this document would be an example of persuasive writing. It is also an example of expository writing, because the author is explaining the concept of global warming.
In that case, this section would meet the requirements from standards W.7.1 and W.7.2: Provide a concluding statement or section that follows from and supports the argument(s) presented.

EXERCISE:

Select a topic for which you can present claims, reasons, evidence and conclusions from two viewpoints. One viewpoint will be in favor of a claim, the other viewpoint will not be in favor of (will be opposed to or against) the claim; this opposition can be expressed as a counterclaim or as a different claim that leads to a different conclusion. You can include as many claims as you like.

Each claim should be supported by at least one reason and one piece of evidence in its favor and should have at least one conclusion. It should include at least one counterclaim and at least one reason and one piece of evidence that leads to a conclusion telling why the counterclaim should not be accepted.

_____

_____

_____

_____

_____
_____
_____
_____
_____
_____
_____
_____
_____
_____
_____
_____
_____
_____
_____
_____
_____
_____

 There are eight standards that this chapter supports.

Three of these standards are designated W.6.1, W.7.1 and W.8.1; the other three are designated W.6.2, W.7.2.and W.8.2 (grades 6 through 8).

Because the wording in each or these two groups of standards is very similar for each grade, the author has decided to use the wording from standards W.7.1 and W.7.2 (grade 7) in this document to show how the content of this document meets the writing standards.

*Each of these standards has several subparagraphs that further define the standard, and these have been inserted into this document to show more specifically how the document meets the standard. These subparagraphs and any author's notes will appear in **bold italic type.***

Footnote 12: Merriam-Webster.com.

Footnote 13: Global Warming Fast Facts, National Geographic News, updated June 14, 2007. http://news.nationalgeographic.com.

Footnote 14: Open Source Systems, Science, Solutions at http://ossfoundation.us/.

XII. Techniques in Action: Stories and Essays Written by Middle School Students

EXERCISE:

(1) Review the stories for writing style, grammar and content.

(2) Look for a variety of different errors the author has made, including redundant text, illogical content, excessive wordiness, punctuation and grammatical errors, and inconsistencies in verb tense and voices.

(3) Use the blank section beside each portion of the story in the COMMENTS column to comment on any errors you see as well as make general comments about the text and content.

These tasks can be completed independently or in a small group setting.

.STORY #1: Jonathan's Adventure

Comment - This is narrative and descriptive writing whose purpose it is to entertain.

STORY	COMMENTS
"Jon, wake up, wake up!" shouted Jon's uncle. "Time for school!" Jon suddenly tumbled out of bed, muttered something under his breath and stormed off to the bathroom.	
Jonathan Burke was the son of Thompson Burke and Mary Burke, the owners of the biggest toy shop in the world. Jon was 11 years old and lived with his uncle, Norris Burke, who was the owner of a large farm in California. Jon's parents looked after Jon until he was 2 years old and could walk. Then his father and mother got the amazing idea of opening the largest toy shop in the world with all the money they had. Once they had started the construction they decided that Jon would be a distraction from their dream and gave him to Jon's uncle, his father's brother, to raise.	
So, Uncle Norris, what's for breakfast?" asked Jon after getting ready as fast as a race horse runs. "Oh nothing much, just some eggs, toast and orange juice." Norris replied. "Ok, then I'll eat quickly and get going," said Jon while shoving some toast into his mouth. Jon always liked going to school, but not to learn or because he liked school, but because he got to ride his horse Penelope to school everyday.	
After about ten minutes of riding he reached the school and was pleased to see his best friend Fredrick Carlson waiting for him in the courtyard. Jon dismounted from his horse and ran over to the courtyard entrance. "Hey Fred," said Jon. "Hey Jon, let's get going, the bell rang 5 minutes ago." And with that they both ran to their class.	

STORY	COMMENTS
The school day was normal; everyone was happy. When the school bell rang at the end of the school day, everyone ran out to the courtyard to say goodbye to their friends. Jon said bye to Fred and a few other people, mounted his horse and took off.	
Jon was halfway across the bridge and he was feeling happy and playful as his horse galloped. Then suddenly, one of the boards on the bridge snapped when Penelope's front hooves landed on it. Penelope lost her balance, and crashed into a wooden side railing. She hit the railing with so much force that it snapped, and she and the railing and Jon flew off the bridge and landed in the water, alive and very scared.	
Jon caught hold of Penelope's reins and he pulled himself onto her. Thank God the water was shallow enough so Penelope's hoofs could reach the bottom and with Jon's urging, she was able to walk out of the river and onto the bank. Jon fell to the ground in disbelief that he was alive and was soaking in the feelings of happiness and joy that he was experiencing right now.	
Then he started to wonder how he was going to get home; he didn't know the route to get back to the bridge.	

STORY	COMMENTS
Penelope walked over to the river and took a sip of the cold water. Jon did the same and patted Penelope affectionately. He was very happy to see her all energized for the long trip back. Then he said, "Hey Penny, how are we going to get back? We don't even know the way?" She whinnied in reply but he could not understand her. A thought occurred to him…why not wait here until someone came along the road, and yell up to them as they crossed the bridge? So he waited and waited but no one came.	
After awhile Jon and Penelope started to shiver.	
Jon decided that he needed to make a fire to keep them warm. He found some dead shreds of bark and some dead branches on the ground in the forest, snapped off some twigs, built a fire and in no time, he and Penelope were warm again.	
As he was doing this he remembered all the lessons that he had learned from his uncle when he was a few years younger: how to make a good bow and arrow to catch meat, how to find the right type of berries, and how to make a fishing rod with nothing more than string, a safety pin and a piece of wood. His uncle made sure that he always had all of this stuff when he went out. At this moment he was more grateful to his uncle then anyone in the world, and wondered what his Uncle Norris was doing. Back at home, Uncle Norris was beginning to worry; it was 7:00 and Jon had not come home.	

STORY	COMMENTS
So Uncle Norris set out to search all of the places where Jon could be. First he went to Fred's house. He wasn't there. Then he went to the public library, Jon wasn't there either. Then he went to the school using a different route, completely avoiding the bridge.	
No one was there. It was quiet and dark; the only thing that Norris could hear was the flag flapping in the wind. He began to shout repeatedly, "Where are you Jon?"	
Meanwhile, back at the bridge, Jon sat there waiting. He didn't know what time it was because he lost his watch when he fell. He and Penelope ate some berries and drank some water for their dinner; he was feeling very sleepy. So he took the saddle off Penelope's back to use it as a pillow. He said, "Good night Pen," and he rubbed her nose. The ground was rocky, so he looked along the edge of the forest where there was some grass that was soft enough for him to sleep on, and which was a place where he could still be seen by someone crossing the bridge.	

STORY	COMMENTS
As soon as he lay down on the grass and put his head on the saddle, he fell into a deep sleep.	
After searching in several places for Jon, Uncle Norris became very frightened and drove to the police station.	
There he asked whether they had seen Jon or a horse pass by any time in the afternoon around 3:00. They all shook their heads. So Uncle Norris filed a missing persons report and requested a search party. The police were very efficient; they had posters and a search party ready within 30 minutes. Uncle Norris was ready to do whatever it took to find his nephew and bring him home. They searched all night, all over the town. It was 1:00 in the morning when they decided to call it a night and start searching again in the morning.	
Until then Uncle Norris would just have to wait and see whether Jon would come home on his own.	
After sleeping a few hours, a nightmare woke Jon up. He had dreamt that he was falling again, but this time the water was very deep and he was drowning and couldn't breathe. The rest of the night Jon couldn't sleep; he lay there on the forest floor, looking up at the starry sky.	

STORY	COMMENTS
At 6:25 the next morning, everyone was searching for Jon again except Uncle Norris, who was sitting in the police station trying to think of other places Jon could be. Then it hit him, "THE BRIDGE!"	
As soon as he thought of it he ran out the door, got into his car and raced off toward the bridge. One of the police officers was curious as to where Uncle Norris was going in such a hurry, and followed him. Suddenly Norris stopped his car and got out. He saw the gap where the railing had been and was wondering what had happened to the bridge.	
He screamed, "JON, JON!!!! WHERE ARE YOU?" Jon was lying there in a drowsy daze. Was someone calling his name? He sat up, then walked slowly to the edge of the forest and looked up at the bridge. He saw a figure, and although he couldn't see it well in the pre-dawn light, it looked like his Uncle Norris	

STORY	COMMENTS
"UNCLE NORRIS! UNCLE NORRIS! DOWN HERE!" He screamed. "JON, OH JON. THANK GOD! JUST WAIT FOR A LITTLE BIT; WE WILL GET A LADDER DOWN TO YOU!" Uncle Norris shouted. They were both so happy that they had found each other. The policeman who had followed Uncle Norris radioed for a fire truck, and shortly after the truck arrived, the firemen lowered a ladder to Jon, who climbed up to join them on the bridge. The policeman also called a veterinarian, who arrived and gave Penelope a sedative. The fire truck had a rescue sling, which they lowered and with the veterinarian's help, fastened it around Penelope's belly, and the firemen hauled her in the sling up to the bridge.	
Jon was so relieved! He promised his uncle that he would always take another route to school and avoid that bridge.	

STORY #2: A Servant's Freedom

Comment: This is narrative writing whose purpose it is to entertain.

STORY	COMMENTS
Often late at night when there are people walking around the streets of Spain, I lay asleep in my bed, hoping that one day I would be able to be free like them. I lay in bed hoping that one day I would be able to get a job that was outside of that big house that I stayed in, and that the salary would be better than what I was getting then.	
This wish of mine came true, but it was long after I made this wish and it was long after a lot of sneaking around escaping from the house when no one was there and making sure that I was back in time to make everything for the horrible family that owned me. This was my life, and this is the story of how I found a job very far from the family that owned me, a job where there was better salary and a job where I was allowed to be free and roam where I wanted to. This is the story of my struggle and the way life was when I was a young boy	
It was twelve o'clock in the afternoon and I could hear the traffic of all of the horns honking and all of the people yelling in Spanish	
I was washing the dishes when the mistress walked into the kitchen, and said "Dobby! What is this? What is this? My clothes have been washed but they have not been IRONED!!!! Do it now or you will be punished!" She yelled. So I washed my hands, dried them, and then walked to her room with her dress in my hand, ironed it quickly then got back to my work.	

STORY	COMMENTS
This was my life every single day, and I was almost used to it. It was the beatings from the gardener that I could not bear even now. That is why my policy was never to disobey any order from the master or the mistress, just so that I would not have to have any beatings. But was this policy enough? No it was not. Whenever I did not do exactly what they wanted me to do, in the exact manner, then I would get punished. Over time I learned how to do things and how to make the master, mistress and their sons happy.	
There are only two good things that I remember from living in that house	
They were Jimmy the dog and my owners' only daughter, who was the kindest of all of them and showed some sympathy for me. There is more about her later in the story. Jimmy was one of my favorites because we were both brought to the house together and we both grew up as if we were brothers. None of the family members liked him, for they thought that he looked ugly. This was the first time that I got the courage to ask for something from my owners. When I asked them if I could have the dog they were about to hit when their daughter came in the middle of the fight and said that if it was something that they didn't want then why would they think twice before giving it away to someone who wanted it? Her parents looked at each other and then decided that only because they didn't want it, they would let me keep it in my room and it was allowed to roam around the house at its free will as I was, however it was as I was, forbidden to leave the house without removing its collar. I was not allowed to leave the house at all.	

STORY	COMMENTS
I served the family for five long and dreadful years. There were times where	
I remember feeling as if this job was the worst and then there were also times where I remember feeling that the job was not so bad. Then one night I was staring at the sealing of the kitchen which was where I slept. Then I looked at the back door An idea struck me	
Why couldn't I escape from the house through the back door when the family was gone and then come back when before the family had returned?	
Once I found a job I could tell the family and see what they said and also offer to give them all of the possessions that they had provided me with and then leave so that I would not have any debt to them at all. For a whole year I struggled to find a proper job that would let me stay there, roam around during my free time, and also have a better salary.	
Finally I found a job in an inn where the owner was very kind and I found that there was a small room that was fit for me and Jimmy and I could roam where I want.	

STORY	COMMENTS
The salary was almost the same but a little better and it had everything else that I wanted	
The next day I went and told my owner's daughter about what my plan was and she said that it was worth a try.	
So after dinner, I went to my master's office where he was sitting and reading the newspaper. I knelt on my knee and asked him very politely, "Master?" "Humph?" He replied. "Master, I wish to leave this house and find a new job for myself sir." "WHAT? Why would you want to do that now? Have we mistreated you have	
we not provided everything that is necessary for your survival?" he asked. "Yes master, but I would like to change my occupation as it has been five years of my service if it is alright with you then I will take me leave sir." I said. "Have you found a job?" "No sir, I am not allowed to leave the house."	
"So then how will you survive when you are looking for a job?" he asked.: "As I once did sir, by begging from house to house for food and some shelter for one night then everyday I will go and look for a job until I have found one that suites me." I told him. "I may agree however your mistress will be reluctant. If you can find one more boy or girl that is as efficient as you then you will be allowed to leave from your service." "But sir, I am not to leave the house." I said.	

STORY	COMMENTS
The Master looked at the ceiling and then spoke,	
"I will send one guard to give you two hours a day to look for a girl or boy to replace you. Once your two hours is *[are]* up then you will return to this house and finish all of your chores. Do you understand?" his last few words were a very dark and serious "Yes sir, as you say." I left the room in a very happy mood.	
For the next 5 months I looked for the replacement.	
During this time not any insult of even beating could depress me. I was so happy. I found a girl that could take my place. When I found her I felt sorry for her that she accepted, even though I told her all of the difficulties that she would have to face when she was at the house. She still accepted for the offer, saying that she would take on any job that did not require her to be literate*[,]* as she was desperate for money. Then she went to the house and I took my leave. I left with all of my personal belongings too. Once I started living and working at the inn my life was paradise. I was happy because I had enough money to spend on things I had all of the food that I wanted when I wanted for free.	
My room was a bit smaller but all the freedom that I enjoyed during my free time more than made up for the smaller living space. This was the life that I was waiting for. This is what I had worked for those long five years. I just hope that the small little girl that took my place will think of a way to escape when she is ready.	

STORY #3: A Very Cute Intruder

Comment: This is narrative and descriptive writing whose purpose it is to entertain.

STORY	COMMENTS
"Oh, how gross, Monkey. Come on - stop licking me!" said Molly as she opened her eyes. It was 2:30 in the morning and Monkey was trying to wake her up. He looked scared and as soon as Molly looked into his eyes she knew that something was wrong.	
Suddenly she heard something fall in the living room. She thought there must be a stranger in the house because her mother would never wake up in the middle of the night.	
She got up and put her slippers on, got Monkey's metal chain from her bookshelf and called to Monkey "Lead the way Monk." Monkey got up and started to walk very slowly, sniffing the ground for anything unusual.	
When they reached the living room, Monkey stopped and looked back and then Molly came towards him.	
She scanned the living room to see if anyone was there, but there was no one in sight.	

STORY	COMMENTS
Then BAM! A noise came from the kitchen! She walked over towards the kitchen door, and with her hands trembling, slowly, quietly opened it.	
"Awe, your so cute!" she said "Ruff Ruff" barked Monkey. "Shut up Monkey! You're gonna wake up mom!" The intruder that Molly was so scared of was a small Golden Retriever puppy, the same breed as Monkey. It was one of the cutest animals that Molly had ever seen in her life.	
It looked hungry so Molly got some biscuits out of the pantry and placed some on the floor. Then she picked up the puppy and brought it to her room.	
"OK Monkey, you have to take care of the puppy tonight and in the morning we have to somehow convince mom to keep it, got it?" Molly asked. "Ruff" he barked in reply, "Good. Now go to sleep."	
"AAAAHHHHHAHHHHAHAHHAHAHHA-HAH[!!]" Molly fell out of bed to the shrill scream of her mother. She ran to the kitchen where her mother was staring in disbelief. "Ma what happened?" she asked panting. Monkey walked into the kitchen and made a puppy face at Molly's mom.	
"Molly, who is this?" Molly's mother said pointing at the puppy. Molly took a good look around the now destroyed kitchen	

STORY	COMMENTS
"Please don't tell me that you went out and found yourself another dog, because we don't have any space in the house to keep this thing." "I didn't go and find the dog. It must have gotten got into the house through Monkey's doggy door!	
Last night at around 3:00 a.m. I heard a noise and I thought someone had broken into the house, and when I went to see who it was, I found this cute thing with its nose in Monkey's bowl, trying to get some food." she explained. "So what do we do now? Do you want me to keep it?" Mom asked. "Well my birthday is coming in five days, so this could be an early and only present." Molly said. " OK, that does make sense, but there are some rules. You have to keep one dog in the house and the other in the barn. If I were you I would raise the young one in the house, and when it gets older, keep both of them in the barn. Also, you have to do everything to take care of it; only bother me for food and necessary supplies. If you agree to follow these rules the dog is yours." said Molly's mother. Molly jumped up and gave her mother a big hug! Molly was so happy! "Thank you! Thank you! Thank you! Thank you so much! I'm gonna name her Maggi!"	

STORY #4: The Choice

Comment: This is narrative writing whose purpose it is to entertain.

STORY	COMMENTS
BEEP! BEEP! BEEP! sounded the alarm clock in Andy's room. He woke up with a start and then he yelled "YESSSS." He leaped out of bed and began jumping up and down and shouting: "Today is the day, today is the day!"	
Andy's mother walked into the room "Wow cowboy, slow down there. Remember - the violin plays soothing music, not heavy metal!" She said. So with this hint So in response, Andy began to dance a ballet, and his mother began to laugh. "Okay, come on, brush your hair, shower, and come downstairs with your bag for breakfast. Oh, and did you finish your homework last night?" his mother asked. while she walked out the door. "Yes mom, all of it." Andy replied. "Be down in a flash." and so he was.	
Andy was in third grade and today was the day that Andy's class got to choose the instrument that they wanted to learn on for the rest of their school year. Ever since Andy knew that this day would come he was set on learning the violin because that's what his grandmother used to play when she was his age. After finishing a quick bowl of cereal, Andy rushed to the car. and sat down with his seatbelt fastened. "Mom, come on let's go! We're going to be late!" Andy screamed. "Andy, let Peter put his shoes on just one more minute!" Andy got his wish and they all were sitting in the car.	

STORY	COMMENTS
"Dad wished you good luck for the big day when he called this morning," Andy's mother said. "He also said that Ireland has a good luck pool where he put a coin for you." Andy said really excited.	
Then Andy's mom parked the car. and then all got down. As soon as Andy hit the ground with his Nike sneakers he gave his mom a big hug and ran right straight for the door. As soon as he walked into the school he saw his music teacher, and he said "Good Morning Mrs. Musinca." "Oh Good Mooooorning Andy."	
"Are you ready to pick your instrument today?" the kind teacher asked. "Oh yes ma'am I have been waiting for a long time. I want to pick the violin." he said excitedly. Mrs. Musinca nodded, winked, then walked away. Then Andy heard the bell ring so he hurried off to his classroom. He stopped at the door where the sign 33 hung and peered inside to see if everyone had come already there were still some empty seats and people were putting their backpacks away. He knew that he was on time so he walked in casually. The teacher, Mr. Gates, stood and said "Good Morning kids. Okay, you guys know the drill, let's say the Pledge of Allegiance," and then all of the kids started "I pledge allegiance to the flag of the united states of America and to the republic for which it stands one nation under god, indivisible and with liberty and justice for all."	
"Thank you students, you all are getting better day by day when it comes to saying the Pledge together as one voice."	

STORY	COMMENTS
"Um, what special class do we have today?" Mr. Gates asked. "WE HAVE MUSIC" They all chorused. "That's right! But first let's finish with our math and other subjects. Today we are going to work on Geometry. How many of you forgot to get your geo boards today?" questioned the teacher. None of the students raised their hands. "EXCELLENT!" Mr. Gates exclaimed. So the day went on like this and the students kept Mr. Gates in a very good mood. Soon enough the lunch bell rang; everyone had been waiting for this because right after the lunch period the students would go to the music room!	
All of the students of room 33 had finished their lunches very quickly and were waiting for the bell to ring *[and]* Once they heard that bell ring they all got up and they were jumping up and down for Mrs. Musinca to arrive. When she finally got there she had a big smile on her face."OKAY EVERYONE, LINE UP" she yelled, and at once all of the students lined up in single file. She then gave the command "FORWARD MARCH" and twenty pairs of small legs marched to the music room As soon as they walked into the room, they were all very excited but made sure that they stayed in the line only because it was one of the 'must follow rules' in the class room. 'Never fall out of line until told to.'	
Mrs. Musinca went to her desk and pulled out an attendance sheet. "Now each student will be called one by one and he or she will tell me what they want to play from the spot where they are standing now. You have to give me your choice from the list that is behind you, and make sure that it is there.	

STORY	COMMENTS
Then the calling began, "Andrew" she called "The cello" he replied. "Marvelous choice." She said. "Andy" she called "Violin." he replied cheerfully. "A high spirited instrument for a high spirited boy." she said. After the last name was called, the students calling went on and on and then in the end a boy named Zang was called and he picked the saxophone and then they all were very anxious to see what their teacher would do. Then She said "Well, what now. Hmmmmm I think that I am going to give you all a little time to examine the instruments that you have chosen. The school has rented many instruments for you as the parents instructed. So you may look at the instrument that they have gotten you and then you can take it home when you have brought the money for this year." Then with a nod from every one she called all of the names and told them to come forth while handing them the right instrument and size that was ordered for them.	
She called Andrew, and he went to her desk, and Mrs. Musinca wrote his name on a tag and tied it to the handle of a violin case. Then she held it out and said: "Take care of it, Andy. It is really special."	

STORY #5: A Stressful Change

Comment: This is narrative and descriptive writing whose purpose it is to entertain.

STORY	COMMENTS
It was a fine August afternoon and fall would soon be closing in on the small town of Piscataway. Lyra Robinson and her parents had landed at JFK International airport after a very long flight from Australia. Lyra was going into 4th grade. She wasn't so excited about this move, but it came about because Lyra's father had been promoted to team leader at a company called American Standards. Lyra was proud of her dad for getting a job here but she was upset that they had to move just for the job. Eventually her mother got her to understand that if they didn't move, they would be away from daddy for a very long time. So, reluctantly, she accepted the necessity for the move, and here they were in a taxicab heading from the airport to their newly purchased house.	
THUD! THUD! The taxi went over a speed bump and woke her from a deep sleep. "Lyra dearie, welcome to our new home!" her mother said in an excited voice. As much as Lyra did not like to admit it, the house was beautiful, full of greenery around it, and on the door was the bold golden number 23. Lyra looked at her watch and it was already 10:00 in the morning. She said in a frantic voice: "Mum, Mum where are all of the kids here? I don't see anyone riding bikes or doing anything. It looks so boring; it looks like it's a place for old people to hang out." She cried "Now now Lyra, you must not judge a place by the first look, okay? Now lets go inside the house and start unpacking." Then her mother turned back to see Lyra's father sleeping as well. "Well am I the only one who didn't sleep in the car? Jim wake up now!" She yelled. "Mary what is it?" Jim said. "We reached the house Jim. Look at it, so beautiful." Then her father got up and said, "Okay, come on out of the car, we got a big day ahead of us, lets go go go!".	

STORY	COMMENTS
Her parents' comments ignited a happy spirit inside Lyra. The Robinsons were ready to do anything today. Lyra jumped out of the car to feel the sun on her face; it was such a beautiful place to live in. Lyra had imagined that the place would be like a dump, but now she could see it was bigger and better than the small apartment they had back in Australia. Then there was a huge sound in behind her Then she heard the loud sound of a trailer truck engine and airbrakes. When she turned around there was a huge 18 wheel tractor trailer truck that had just pulled up to their house. With the sound of the brakes finally ending Lyra's father went over to the back waiting for the driver to come and open the door for him. By the time that the truck driver had opened all of the locks on the truck's loading doors, Lyra's mom had opened the front door and the garage doors. Soon all of the boxes were being carried toward the house. Lyra was so bored that she started to help her mother. They both worked together to open everything from the plastic wrap and make sure that nothing was broken, especially the collection of little handmade dolls that were made by Lyra's mother.	
By the time it was 3:00 in the afternoon, Lyra was poofed worn out and asked her mom to make some lunch. The only problem was, they didn't know where to call for restaurants or delis that would deliver, which they needed since they did not have a car. Then Lyra's mother got an idea. "Hey why don't we go and ask one of our neighbors. They might know some place where we could get some food, right?" she asked. "Of course we would" said a voice at the front door. There were two adults and two kids; one of the children looked very small and was very adorable. "Why yes you did, so let me guess - you are from Australia right?" Meena asked. "Rightiyo" said Jim. "Well I couldn't help but overhear - you guys are having some trouble with ordering lunch, right? Well how about we take you out for lunch, and please don't say no. It is our way of welcoming you to the town," said Meena.	

STORY	COMMENTS
"Oh thank you so much - yes I think that we would like to have some lunch, and we would be able to get to know you too." said Mary. So Lyra and her parents went out to lunch with their new neighbors. They were very nice people and Lyra liked them a lot. The rest of the day went smoothly and they were able to unpack almost everything. Then Lyra remembered that she had school tomorrow, and suddenly she became worried about what was going to happen then. But the only thing she could do was wait.	
The next day, Lyra woke up at six o'clock and got ready for school. Her mother had packed her favorite food, pasta with some cilantro on top. She went to the bus stop with her father. The school bus came. "Okay darling, now be good in school, got it?" her father asked. Lyra nodded 'yes', gave him a hug and then ran for the bus. When she got on the bus there were all these friendly faces smiling at her, looking eager to become friends with her. She then remembered that Kavin was also going to be on the same bus, so she looked for him and when he came right behind her, he said: "Hey Lyra, move back so we can sit together." She smiled and then the two new friends moved over to the back of the bus. Then the bus started to move and all of the students on the bus were chatting with their friends and rejoicing after two months of holidays – everyone, that is, except for Lyra; she was worried about what school would be like for her.	
Once they reached the school Kavin led Lyra to classroom 27 and then said bye and went to. his own classroom. From here on it was going to be Lyra on her own. She took a deep breath and then she took one step into the classroom.	

STORY	COMMENTS
She was surprised at how happy the kids were and the jolly feeling that she got as soon as she walked into the room. Then someone tapped her on the back and said "Excusem Moi." She turned around to see the smiling face of her teacher. "You must be Lyra, am I right?" she asked. Lyra nodded shyly. "My name is Mrs. Hutchinson, how are you today?" "I am fine Mrs. Hutchinson." Lyra said. Mrs. Hutchinson went to her desk, and said "Good morning students!" The whole room fell silent, but then they all said "Good Morning Mrs Hutchinson!" followed by the Pledge of Allegiance. Lyra didn't know the Pledge, so she just stood with her right hand on her heart. Then they all sat down and then Mrs. Hutchinson stood up. "Today I am seeing many familiar faces, but I don't know your names, so let's start by introducing ourselves, starting with I think it best for us to start from the newest member of our school, Lyra. She is the pretty little girl sitting right over there. Sweetie, stand up and say your name and where you are from; the rest of you can just say your names." Lyra said. "Hi, um my name is Lyra and I am from Australia." For some reason everyone clapped and then she sat down. By the time all 28 students had said their names, Lyra had memorized their faces and first names. Once the introductions were done, the teacher didn't start with the lessons; instead, she passed out folders and then she showed the students where everything was in the school.	
When they got back to the classroom she showed them where all the books should be kept and how the classroom should be utilized. Lyra was very happy throughout the day, especially while she was eating lunch with her new friends Rajeena and Trudy. They were really nice and were on Lyra's bus.	

STORY	COMMENTS
Time flew by and Lyra was so busy and enjoying school that she didn't even realize when it was time to go home. She said bye to Mrs. Hutchinson and then she called over to Trudy and Rajeena, and they both walked with her to their bus. It was a fun day for Lyra and she just couldn't wait to tell her mom what had happened. about her first day at school.	

STORY #6: The Night Before Christmas

Comment: This is narrative and descriptive writing whose purpose it is to entertain and to provide an example of a flashback.

STORY	COMMENTS
It was Christmas eve, the twenty fourth of December, and Ron was looking at the night sky from the balcony of his room. He could hear the fire crackling in the hearth while he was staring at the twinkling blanket of stars above him. There was a slight breeze, which made him realize that it was a bit too cold for him to watch the twinkling sky much longer.	
He walked into the room and went to the hall to see that his children, Anna and Jacob, were still awake, and were helping his wife Roseina decorate their lovely Christmas tree. He took a few steps down the hall and then he saw paper that was lying on the stair's landing. The piece of paper revealed to be a photo of Ron's family all having fun and putting up their Christmas tree on Christmas Eve. Ron slowly walked back to his room and sank into his bed, still holding the photo remembering that day so many years ago so vividly that it was almost as if it was going on right in front of his eyes.	
"Ronny be careful with that sweetie; it is made of glass and it might brake" said Ron's mother. "Okay mom, I won't brake it. But what is it? It looks like two birds with the same body." Ron said. "How can two birds have the same body? That's not possible" said Mareena, Ron's older sister. "It doesn't look that way to me; I think they just made it look like that so they could sell the ornament as one whole piece." said Ron's older brother Johnny.	

STORY	COMMENTS
Then their mother said: "Ronny is right; on this matter the two heads represent two doves or two friends and the one body says that they are always friends and that they are connected through a special bond that will never break or die." She stopped with a smile then looked at all of them. "It can be compared to the bond between brothers and sisters and even if they fight and have rough times, they will always stay together. That is the way that I want all of you to be. No matter what comes your way, you all have to stand together."	
[Ron's imaginary trip into the past ended when] suddenly Roseina came into the room, "Whatya got there?" She came across the room and took the photo from Ron's hand. She saw it and smiled.Whenever I look at this photo I remember my childhood and how I used to put up the tree with my mother when I was little.	
Time flies so fast that I still feel like it was yesterday when I was putting up the tree with the help of my brothers, and now I am putting up a tree with my own children." Ron just smiled and was thinking the same thing. Then she gave him a hug and said "Come downstairs; we need your help in putting the star on the top of the tree." Then Ron got up and said "Let's go !"	

STORY #7: A Day in a Life of Conackamack Middle School

Comment: This is narrative and descriptive writing whose purpose it is to entertain and provide examples of the story within a story, intentional misspelling and onomatopoeia writing techniques.

STORY	COMMENTS
"RRRRRRIIIIIIIIIIINNNNNNNNGGGGGGG" went the bell at the end of 3rd period. I walked out of class thinking what I had next period MATH ! -- my least favorite subject! What was I going to do this time to occupy myself during class? During my last math class I ate my lunch and then bought something else during lunch break and then the class before that I took Ruchit's phone and started to play Angry Birds. Today Ruchit is absent and mom gave me some money to buy lunch in the cafeteria because she is sick, but I bought something and ate it already, so all I can do to pass the time in Math class is daydream.	
I sat for the first five minutes of the class Mr. Hickson's voice was so droopy that I was dozing off in my chair, as hard as I tried not to. Eventually my partner and the person sitting in front of me both fell asleep. Then I remembered that last night I stayed up late studying for the English test that I had this morning. That is why I am feeling so tired! Maybe it won't hurt to rest my eyes for a little bit. But the second I closed my eyes I was in a deep sleep that I thought no one except for my mom and her raging voice could bring me out of. After a few minutes of being asleep the dream started.	
It was very dark and the only thing that was visible was a chalkboard and the walls of a room that looked very familiar to me. It was my math classroom and then suddenly there was the math teacher who appeared out of thin air.	

STORY	COMMENTS
"Well, well Hickson, looks like you decided to show up after all, didn't you" someone said. To my surprise it was me who was talking so rudely to my former math teacher, who was now my student. The dream continued in my mind	
"I am sorry that I am late sir, I was brushing my teeth." he said in a frightful voice.	
"That is no excuse, Hickson," I said. "You know that the rule says: 'If you are more than five minutes late to class, I have to send you to the Assistant Principal's office.' So, when this class ends, you are to go there, and here is the slip he will sign that you will return to me showing that you actually went." "But, but, that is not fair! I object! You have no right..." he shouted.	
"I guess you also forgot that you are not to argue with your teacher. Because you did, I am assigning you a math problem that you need to solve and give me the answer after your next study period today." I said. "No, I won't do it. Math is so boring the way you teach it." he said.	
"Yes, you will do it or I'll give you detention. Here is the problem, write it down: Take the square root of 45, and to it add 2.5 to the fifth power, and to that add 16.3 divided by .043, and write out the answer".Suddenly I woke up. Delightfully I found that the classroom was still very bright. The bell rang and as I was walking outside. I thought that the dream was actually quite a satisfying one.	

 The stories in this chapter are examples of:

Writing: W.6.1,6.3,7.1,7.3,8.1,8.3.

Language: L.6.1,6.2,6.3,6.5,7.1,7.2,7.3,7.5,8.1,8.2,8.3,8.5.

XIII Answers

Chapter II

In these answers, redundant text has a strikethrough (cross out) line through it and text added by the editor is enclosed in brackets [ ].

1.1 "Maggi, come on good girl, wake up, come on, you have ~~got~~ to wake up!" Molly said [to her dog]. It was 8:00 in the morning ~~and Molly was trying to wake up Maggi, her dog.~~
Comments: The word "got" is unnecessary. The last phrase is redundant; it is obvious from the first sentence that Molly is trying to wake Maggi up.

1.2 "I have to call this lady and tell her that I found her dog and she can come and pick her up." Molly said, as she turned and walked slowly toward the phone. RING RING RING "Good Morning. Carrie Lendwood speaking." ~~said the lady on the other end of the phone.~~
Comments: From the first sentence, the reader knows that Molly is going to call the dog's owner, so it is redundant to say "rang the phone in Maggi's owner's house." Similarly, when Carrie answers the phone, the reader already knows that Carrie is the lady on the other end of the phone, so the phrase "said the lady…phone is unnecessary

1.3 "Take a look at this dog collar." Molly said. Her mother took the collar ~~from her hands~~ and tried to read it, "The letters are too small. Hand me my reading glasses*[;]*they are right there in the drawer." ~~her mother asked~~. Molly ~~ran over to the drawer~~ grabbed the glasses and ~~without even closing the drawer back~~ ran back to her mother's side.
Comment: Unnecessary words have been struck through. A semicolon has been added [;] to separate two sentences that had been combined into one (the brackets are there only to make sure you see the semicolon).

1.4 An elderly women opened the door and *[rasped]* ~~screamed at the top of her weak lungs~~: "Oh my baby, where had you gone, your mother was furious with me!"
Comment: Because the author said her lungs are weak, then the word "rasped"(to utter with a grating sound) is a better word than "screamed." The author should end the sentence with rasped and delete the phrase "screamed …weak lungs.".

1.5 Andy was in third grade and today was the day that Andy's class *[will]* ~~got to~~ choose their very own special instruments that they wanted to learn for the rest of their school year. Ever since Andy knew that this day would come he ~~was set on learning~~ *[had chosen]* the violin because that's what his grandmother used to play when she was his age. Then he took the bow that was carefully placed inside the case and ~~then he~~ held the violin like his grandmother had shown him, ~~he placed~~ [placing] his chin

on the ~~black color thing which was called the~~ chinrest.
Comment: Unnecessary words have been struck through, and replacements added in brackets [ ].
"Color thing" does not adequately describe a part of the violin, but chinrest does, so the phrase
"color thing which was called the" can be deleted.

1.6 After *[quickly]* finishing a ~~quick~~ bowl of cereal …
Comment: A bowl cannot be quick or slow, but Andy can be quick or slow in eating the cereal.

1.7 The second I closed my eyes I was in a deep sleep that I thought no one could bring me out of. After a few minutes ~~of being asleep~~ I began to dream.
Comment: "of being asleep" is redundant; the prior sentence already tells the reader that the character is asleep.

Chapter III
1.1 Handheld portable phones had not been invented in the 1800's.
1.2 The Golden Gate Bridge is in San Francisco, California, not New York City.
1.3 In 1941, there were only rotary phones, not touch tone phones, and 911 service was not available.
1.4 Television and CNN programming had not been invented yet. Television was introduced in the late 1950's.
1.5 Wifi had not been introduced in 2005.

Chapter VIII
Sight: 15 hash marks. Observation of great location on the highway; condition of sign; paint peeling on exterior walls; trash in parking lot; garbage cans visible from parking lot; holes in carpet; peeling wallpaper; dim lighting; chairs and tables worn, outdated and stained; menu paper; menu contents; cleanliness of kitchen; peeling wallpaper in kitchen; food presentation; portion sizes.

Hearing: 3 hash marks. Conversations with the owner and manager; noise from customers' conversations; noise from local radio station.

Touch: 2 hash marks. Utensils used to test the consistency of the food; fingers used to test the consistency of the food.

Smell: 3 hash marks. Smell from garbage cans; smell of food inside kitchen; smell of food at the table .

Taste: 1 hash mark. Tasting the samples of food.

Chapter XII.

An editor has inserted comments on the author's writing style, grammar and content in all of the stories in this chapter. The comments have identified several kinds of errors that the author has made, including redundant text, illogical content, excessive wordiness, punctuation and grammatical errors, and inconsistencies in verb tenses and voices. The editor's comments are displayed like this: **Comment: This is what a comment looks like.** Also, the editor has entered strikethrough lines through redundant text and replaced some text, which is shown as follows: *[bold italicized text between brackets]*.

The editor's comments also identified positive things about a story, such as well-written introductions, transitions when changing time periods and physical locations, indications of time passing, expressions of a character's emotions, use of descriptive language, correct use of punctuation such as semicolons and colons, use of figures of speech such as similes and personification and logical content.

.STORY #1: Jonathan's Adventure

STORY	COMMENTS
"Jon, wake up, wake up!" shouted Jon's uncle. "Time for school!" Jon suddenly tumbled out of bed, muttered something under his breath and stormed off to the bathroom.	*The emotions "muttered" and "stormed" communicate reluctance and annoyance.* *[W6.3.4, 7.3.4, 8.3.4]*
Jonathan Burke was the son of Thompson Burke and Mary Burke, the owners of the biggest toy shop in the world. Jon was 11 years old and lived with his uncle, Norris Burke, who was the owner of a large farm in California. Jon's parents looked after Jon until he was 2 years old and could walk. Then his father and mother got the amazing idea of opening the largest toy shop in the world with all the money they had. Once they had started the construction they decided that Jon would be a distraction from their dream and gave him to Jon's uncle, his father's brother, to raise.	*This introductory paragraph is well done. It introduces the two main characters, establishes their relationship to each other, and explains why Jon lives with his uncle and not his parents.* *[W6.3.1, 7.3.1, 8.3.1]*
So, Uncle Norris, what's for breakfast?" asked Jon after getting ready as fast as a race horse runs. "Oh nothing much, just some eggs, toast and orange juice." Norris replied. "Ok, then I'll eat quickly and get going," said Jon while shoving some toast into his mouth. Jon always liked going to school, but not to learn or because he liked school, but because he got to ride his horse Penelope to school everyday.	*Author uses a simile here.* *[L6.5.1, 7.5.1, 8.5.1]* *Author introduces the third main character, Jon's horse, and sets up the main action in the story which will occur while he is riding his horse home from school.* *[W6.3.1, 7.3.1, 8.3.1.]*
After about ten minutes of riding he reached the school and was pleased to see his best friend Fredrick Carlson waiting for him in the courtyard. Jon dismounted from his horse and ran over to the courtyard entrance. "Hey Fred," said Jon. "Hey Jon, let's get going, the bell rang 5 minutes ago." And with that they both ran to their class.	*Redundant phrase. The reader understands that it is the horse Jon is dismounting from.*

STORY	COMMENTS
The school day was normal; everyone was happy. When the school bell rang at the end of the school day, everyone ran out to the courtyard to say goodbye to their friends. Jon said bye to Fred and a few other people, mounted his horse and took off.	*To show the passage of time, author says "the school day was normal"; "rang at the end of the school day"; "say goodbye." To show a transition in action from the school yard setting, "mounted his horse and took off"* *[W6.3.3, 7.3.3, 8.3.3.]*
Jon was halfway across the bridge and he was feeling happy and playful as his horse galloped. Then suddenly, one of the boards on the bridge snapped when Penelope's front hooves landed on it. Penelope lost her balance, and crashed into a wooden side railing. She hit the railing with so much force that it snapped, and she and the railing and Jon flew off the bridge and landed in the water, alive and very scared.	*Emotions expressed: "happy" and "playful", although the author should have described how Jon acted while he was happy and playful (show the reader) and not just used the single word expressions (tell the reader)* *Emotions expressed: very scared.* *[W6.3.4, 7.3.4, 8.3.4]*
Jon caught hold of Penelope's reins and he pulled himself onto her. Thank God the water was shallow enough so Penelope's hoofs could reach the bottom and with Jon's urging, she was able to walk out of the river and onto the bank. Jon fell to the ground in disbelief that he was alive and was soaking in the feelings of happiness and joy that he was experiencing right now.	*Emotions expressed: happiness and joy. Author should have explained the reasons for the feelings.* *[W6.3.4, 7.3.4, 8.3.4]*
Then he started to wonder how he was going to get home; he didn't know the route to get back to the bridge.	*The author uses a semicolon in the preceding sentence to connect two closely related events.*

STORY	COMMENTS
Penelope walked over to the river and took a sip of the cold water. Jon did the same and patted Penelope affectionately. He was very happy to see her all energized for the long trip back. Then he said, "Hey Penny, how are we going to get back? We don't even know the way?" She whinnied in reply but he could not understand her. A thought occurred to him…why not wait here until someone came along the road, and yell up to them as they crossed the bridge? So he waited and waited but no one came.	*These events could be written as two separate sentences, but using a semicolon indicates that these events are very closely related. The part of the sentence that precedes the semicolon makes the statement "he started to wonder how he was going to get home." The part that follows the semicolon tells why he was wondering about how to get home "he didn't know the route to get back to the bridge."* *In the preceding paragraph, the author uses very descriptive words that paint a picture of the action in the reader's mind. The action takes place in logical order.*
After awhile Jon and Penelope started to shiver.	*Time passing is demonstrated* *"waited and waited" and "After awhile."* *[W6.3.3, 7.3.3, 8.3.3.]*
Jon decided that he needed to make a fire to keep them warm. He found some dead shreds of bark and some dead branches on the ground in the forest, snapped off some twigs, built a fire and in no time, he and Penelope were warm again.	*The author uses very descriptive words that paint a picture in the reader's mind.* *[W6.3.4, 7.3.4, 8.3.4.]*
As he was doing this he remembered all the lessons that he had learned from his uncle when he was a few years younger: how to make a good bow and arrow to catch meat, how to find the right type of berries, and how to make a fishing rod with nothing more than string, a safety pin and a piece of wood. His uncle made sure that he always had all of this stuff when he went out. At this moment he was more grateful to his uncle then anyone in the world, and wondered what his Uncle Norris was doing. Back at home, Uncle Norris was beginning to worry; it was 7:00 and Jon had not come home.	*The colon introduces a list of phrases telling what the lessons he remembered were about.* *"Back at home" in the next paragraph is a transition in setting from the woods by the bridge to Uncle Norris' and Jon's home.* *The author uses a semicolon in the preceding sentence to connect two closely related events. These events could be written as two separate sentences, but using a semicolon indicates that these events are very closely related.*

STORY	COMMENTS
	The part of the sentence that precedes the semicolon makes the statement "Uncle Norris was beginning to worry." The part that follows the semicolon tells why he was beginning to worry "it was 7:00 and Jon had not come home."
So Uncle Norris set out to search all of the places where Jon could be. First he went to Fred's house. He wasn't there. Then he went to the public library, Jon wasn't there either. Then he went to the school using a different route, completely avoiding the bridge.	*This explains why he did not find Jon, although you would think Norris would logically have taken the route Jon normally takes to and from school. Maybe some illogical content here.* *[W6.3.1, 7.3.1, 8.3.1. Logical sequence of events.]*
No one was there. It was quiet and dark; the only thing that Norris could hear was the flag flapping in the wind. He began to shout repeatedly, "Where are you Jon?"	*Time passing is indicated by "it was 7:00 and Jon had not come home"; "it was quiet and dark" (it had been light out when Jon started home).* *Comment: "Meanwhile" in the next paragraph is a transition in setting from where Norris was searching to Jon's location in the woods by the bridge.*
Meanwhile, back at the bridge, Jon sat there waiting. He didn't know what time it was because he lost his watch when he fell. He and Penelope ate some berries and drank some water for their dinner; he was feeling very sleepy. So he took the saddle off Penelope's back to use it as a pillow. He said, "Good night Pen," and he rubbed her nose. The ground was rocky, so he looked along the edge of the forest where there was some grass that was soft enough for him to sleep on, and which was a place where he could still be seen by someone crossing the bridge.	*Good logic here in Jon's decision to pick a sleeping spot that was visible from the bridge.*

STORY	COMMENTS
As soon as he lay down on the grass and put his head on the saddle, he fell into a deep sleep.	
After searching in several places for Jon, Uncle Norris became very frightened and drove to the police station.	*Another transition in settings: from the area where Norris was searching to the police station.*
There he asked whether they had seen Jon or a horse pass by any time in the afternoon around 3:00. They all shook their heads. So Uncle Norris filed a missing persons report and requested a search party. The police were very efficient; they had posters and a search party ready within 30 minutes. Uncle Norris was ready to do whatever it took to find his nephew and bring him home. They searched all night, all over the town. It was 1:00 in the morning when they decided to call it a night and start searching again in the morning.	*Transition in time setting from all night to the next morning.* *[W6.3.3, 7.3.3, 8.3.3. Change in time period.]*
Until then Uncle Norris would just have to wait and see whether Jon would come home on his own.	*Another transition in setting from the search locations to the woods by the bridge.*
After sleeping a few hours, a nightmare woke Jon up. He had dreamt that he was falling again, but this time the water was very deep and he was drowning and couldn't breathe. The rest of the night Jon couldn't sleep; he lay there on the forest floor, looking up at the starry sky.	*Comment: The author uses a semicolon in the preceding sentence to connect two closely related thoughts. These thoughts could be written as two separate sentences, but using a semicolon indicates that the thoughts in the sentences are very closely related. The first sentence makes the statement "Jon couldn't sleep." The second sentence states what happens because he couldn't sleep - "he lay there...."* *[W6.3.4, 7.3.4, 8.3.4]*

STORY	COMMENTS
	Another transition in setting and time: from nighttime when Jon lay awake to early the next morning; from the woods near the bridge to the search locations and police station. *[W6.3.3, 7.3.3, 8.3.3.]*
At 6:25 the next morning, everyone was searching for Jon again except Uncle Norris, who was sitting in the police station trying to think of other places Jon could be. Then it hit him, "THE BRIDGE!"	*When unexpected events happen in the plot of a story, like Norris's sudden realization about the bridge, these events are called plot twists, and they change the actions in the plot (now the search turns to the bridge).*
As soon as he thought of it he ran out the door, got into his car and raced off toward the bridge. One of the police officers was curious as to where Uncle Norris was going in such a hurry, and followed him. Suddenly Norris stopped his car and got out. He saw the gap where the railing had been and was wondering what had happened to the bridge.	*Good use of logic here; a prior event, the breaking of the railing, is reintroduced into the story at this later time, and gives Norris an important clue as to where Jon could be.*
He screamed, "JON, JON!!!! WHERE ARE YOU?" Jon was lying there in a drowsy daze. Was someone calling his name? He sat up, then walked slowly to the edge of the forest and looked up at the bridge. He saw a figure, and although he couldn't see it well in the pre-dawn light, it looked like his Uncle Norris	*Speech shown in capital letters and multiple exclamation points indicate shouting or some other loud noise.* *[W6.3.2, 7.3.2, 8.3.2.]* *Comment: The author pointed out earlier in the story that Jon picked a place to sleep that could be seen from the bridge. So why didn't Norris see him now? May be illogical content here.*

STORY	COMMENTS
"UNCLE NORRIS! UNCLE NORRIS! DOWN HERE!" He screamed. "JON, OH JON. THANK GOD! JUST WAIT FOR A LITTLE BIT; WE WILL GET A LADDER DOWN TO YOU!" Uncle Norris shouted. They were both so happy that they had found each other. The policeman who had followed Uncle Norris radioed for a fire truck, and shortly after the truck arrived, the firemen lowered a ladder to Jon, who climbed up to join them on the bridge. The policeman also called a veterinarian, who arrived and gave Penelope a sedative. The fire truck had a rescue sling, which they lowered and with the veterinarian's help, fastened it around Penelope's belly, and the firemen hauled her in the sling up to the bridge.	*[W6.3.2, 7.3.2, 8.3.2.]* *Good, common sense logic and detail here. Because the author had a policeman follow Norris, the policemen had his police radio to call for a fire truck and a veterinarian. Also good logic – fire companies have rescue equipment, such as a sling and ladders, and sedating Penelope makes a lot of sense, since she could have panicked when her hoofs left the ground and she became airborne. However, it would have been more logical for Jon to stay with the horse to make sure she stayed calm and then climb the ladder, instead of leaving the horse alone with the veterinarian.*
Jon was so relieved! He promised his uncle that he would always take another route to school and avoid that bridge.	*Comment: This is the author's conclusion, and it follows logically from the events in the story. However, if the bridge was the shortest route, Jon could dismount and walk Penelope across, especially if the railing was repaired and any rotted floorboards replaced. Also, if this story is set when cell phones were available, Jon could promise to call Norris on his cell phone when he was leaving from or arriving at the school.* *[W6.3.5, 7.3.5, 8.3.5.]* *[W6.3.1, 7.3.1, 8.3.1.]*

STORY #2: A Servant's Freedom

STORY	COMMENTS
Often late at night when ~~there are~~ people [were] walking around the streets of Spain, I [lay awake] ~~lay asleep~~ in my bed, hoping that one day I would be able to be free like them. I lay in bed hoping that one day I would be able to get a job ~~that was outside of that big house that I stayed in~~, *[and live away from this family,]* and that the salary would be better than what I was getting ~~then~~.	*If he were asleep, these thoughts would be dreams, so he must be lying awake. [W6.3.1, 7.3.1, 8.3.1]* *"I lay in bed" is redundant; we already know from the previous sentence that the character is lying in bed.*
This wish of mine *[eventually]* came true, but it was long after I made ~~this wish~~ *[it]*, and it was long after a lot of sneaking around *[and]* escaping from the house when no one was there *[to search for a job,]* and making sure that I was back in time to ~~make everything~~ *[perform all my duties]* for the horrible family that owned me. This was my life, and this is the story of *[my struggle to find]* how I found a job very far from the family *[who]* ~~that~~ owned me, a job ~~where there was~~ *[with a higher]* ~~better~~ salary and *[the chance]* ~~a job where I was allowed~~ to be free ~~and~~ *[to]* roam where I wanted to. This is the story of my struggle and the way life was when I was a young boy	*The last sentence is not necessary; the author has already communicated these thoughts to the reader earlier in this paragraph. However, this is a good introductory paragraph to the story because it lets the reader know the main character's living situation and the problems he is facing in his life, and how he would like to solve these problems.*
It was twelve o'clock in the afternoon and I could hear the traffic of all of the horns honking and all of the people yelling in Spanish	*This sentence is too wordy [W6.3.3, 7.3.3, 8.3.3]*
I was washing the dishes when the mistress *[of the house]* walked into the kitchen, and ~~said~~ *[confronted me with]* "Dobby! What is this? What is this? My clothes have been washed but they have not been IRONED!!!! Do it now or you will be punished!" She yelled. So I washed my hands, dried them, and then walked to her room with her dress in my hand, ironed it quickly then got back to my *[other chores]*~~work~~.	*"confronted me" is more dramatic than "said"* *[W6.3.2, 7.3.2, 8.3.2]*

STORY	COMMENTS
This was *[typical of]* my life every single day, and I was almost used to it. It was the beatings from the gardener that I could not bear even now. That is why my policy was never to disobey any order from the master or the mistress, just so that I would not have to ~~have~~ *[suffer]* any beatings. But was this policy enough? No it was not. Whenever I did not do exactly what they wanted me to do, in the exact manner, then I would get punished. Over time I learned ~~how~~ to do things ~~and how to make the~~ *[in a way that made the]* master, mistress and their sons happy.	*[W6.3.4, 7.3.4, 8.3.4]*
There are only two good things that I remember from living in that house[:]	*Use a colon here because the author is creating a list (of two things that were good).*
~~They were~~ Jimmy the dog and my owners' only daughter, who was the kindest of all of them and showed some sympathy for me. There is more about her later in the story. Jimmy was one of my favorites because we were both brought to the house together and we both grew up as if we were brothers. None of the family members liked him, for they thought *[he was]* ~~that he looked~~ ugly. *[Because of this situation,]* This was the first time that I got the courage to ask for something from my owners. When I asked them if I could have the dog*[;]* they were about to hit *[me]* when their daughter came in the middle of the fight and said that *[since the dog]* ~~if it~~ was something ~~that~~ they didn't want*[,]* ~~then~~ why would they think twice before giving it away to someone who wanted it? Her parents looked at each other and then decided that only because they didn't want it, they would let me keep it in my room and *[that it would be]* ~~it was~~ allowed to *[freely]* roam around the house ~~at its free will as I was, however it was as I was,~~ *[and that I was]* forbidden to *[take it outside]* ~~leave~~ the house without removing its collar. I was not allowed to leave the house at all.	*Because the servant slave was not allowed to leave the house, that means the dog could not leave either, so the above sentence "and that I was forbidden…its collar" should be deleted. This is illogical content. Also, the original wording is awkward and too wordy.* *[W6.3.4, 7.3.4, 8.3.4]*

STORY	COMMENTS
I served the family for five long and dreadful years. There were times ~~where~~ *[when]*	*use "when" for referring to time periods; use "where" when referring to places. [W6.3.3, 7.3.3, 8.3.3]*
I remember feeling as if this job was the worst and then there were also times where I remember feeling that the job was not so bad. Then one night *[while lying in bed in the kitchen (which is where I slept)]* I was staring at the ~~sealing~~ *[ceiling,]* of the kitchen ~~which was where I slept~~. Then I looked at the back door *[and an]* ~~An~~ idea struck me	*Too wordy. Author used two sentences when one reworded sentence does the job. [W6.3.4, 7.3.4, 8.3.4]*
Why couldn't I escape from the house through the back door *[to search for a job]* when the family was gone and then come back ~~when~~ before the family ~~had~~ returned? *[The family left everyday for several hours, during which the children went to school and the parents went to work.]*	*Adding the previous sentence tells the reader that there is a regular period each weekday when the servant slave would have predictable and adequate time to do a job search, in person.*
Once I found a job I could tell the family and see what they said and also offer to give them all of the possessions that they had provided me with and then leave so that I would not have any *[remaining]* debt to them at all. *[when I left.]*	*"let me stay there" is not clear; it could be interpreted as staying at the same family's house, so to be perfectly clear, the author should add: [provide living quarters, the freedom to]*
For a whole year I struggled to find a proper job that would ~~let me stay there~~, roam around during my free time, and also have a better salary.	*We don't need the words "also have"; the author is listing three things about the job that are following the verb "provide". [W6.3.2, 7.3.2, 8.3.2]*
Finally *[the kind owner of]* ~~I found a job in~~ an inn ~~where the owner was very kind and~~ *[hired me as a waiter and provided]* ~~I found that there was~~ a small room that was fit for me and Jimmy and *[allowed me to]* ~~I could~~ roam where I want*[ed to go whenever I was not working]*.	*The original sentence was poorly constructed; awkward phrasing and too many words but not enough explanation – the type of job offered was not even mentioned.*

STORY	COMMENTS
The salary was ~~almost the same but~~ a little better [too.] ~~and it had everything else that I wanted~~	*It is obvious that the job had all three things that the former servant slave wanted, because the author listed them at the beginning of this paragraph, so this phrase "and it had everything else that I wanted" is redundant.*
The next day I went and told my owner's daughter about what my plan was and she said that it was worth a try.	
~~So a~~ [A]fter dinner, I went to my master's office where he was sitting and reading the newspaper. I knelt ~~on my knee~~ [down] and asked him very politely, "Master?" "Humph?" He replied. "Master, I wish to leave this house and find a new job for myself sir." "WHAT? Why would you want to do that now? Have we mistreated you*[? H]*~~h~~ave	*There needs to be a question mark between "you" and "have." The question mark ends the sentence and a capital "H" starts a new sentence.* [W6.3.2, 7.3.2, 8.3.2]
we not provided everything that is necessary for your survival?" he asked. "Yes master, but I would like to change my occupation as it has been five years of my service *[to you, and]* if it is alright with you *[,]* then I will take ~~me~~ *[my]* leave sir." I said. "Have you found a job?" "No sir, *[I lied]* I am not allowed to leave the house."	*Very smart that the author remembered this fact, which he alluded to earlier. If the servant slave had not said this, the master would know the servant slave had left the house, which was against the rules..* [W6.3.2, 7.3.2, 8.3.2]
"So then how will you survive when you are looking for a job?" he asked. *[I again lied]*: "As I once did sir, by begging from house to house for food and some shelter for one night*[. T]*~~t~~hen everyday I will go and look for a job until I have found one that ~~suites~~ *[suits]* me." I told him. "I may agree*[;]* however your mistress will be reluctant. If you can find ~~one more~~ *[a]* boy or girl ~~that~~ *[who]* is as efficient as you then you will be allowed to leave from your service." "But sir, I am not to leave the house." I said.	*Remember, a boy or girl is a who, not a that.* [W6.3.2, 7.3.2, 8.3.2] *Again, very smart that the author remembered this fact, which he alluded to earlier.*

STORY	COMMENTS
The Master *[frowned, put his hand on his chin and stared]* ~~looked~~ at the ceiling and then spoke,	*This is the body language a person might show when he has to focus and think about making a difficult decision*
"I will send one guard ~~to give~~ *[with]* you *[for]* two hours a day to look for ~~a girl or boy~~ *[someone]* to replace you. Once your two hours ~~is~~ *[are]* up then you will return to this house and finish all of your chores. Do you understand?" ~~his last few words were~~ *[he said in]* a very dark and serious *[tone of voice.]* "Yes sir, as you say." I left the room ~~in a very happy mood.~~ *[with a smile on my face and in my heart.]*	*[W6.3.2, 7.3.2, 8.3.2]*
For the next ~~5~~ *[five]* months I looked for the replacement.	*All other numbers in the story have been written out, so to be consistent, write out "five".*
During this time not any insult ~~of~~ *[or]* even *[a]* beating could depress me. I was so happy. I found a girl ~~that~~ *[who]* could take my place. When I found her I felt sorry for her that she accepted, even though I told her all of the difficulties that she would have to face when she was at the house. She still accepted for the offer, saying that she would take on any job that did not require her to be literate*[,]* as she was desperate for money. Then she went to the house and I took my leave. I left with all of my personal belongings too. Once I started living and working at the inn my life was *[a]* paradise. I was happy because I had enough money to spend on things*[,]* I had all of the food that I wanted*[,]* when I wanted*[,]* for free.	*The author is thorough in that he not only said the servant slave was happy, he explained why he was happy.*
My room was a bit smaller *[than the space I had had in the kitchen of the former house]* but all the freedom that I enjoyed during my free time more than made up for the smaller living space. This was the life that I was waiting for. This is what I had worked for those long five years. I just hope that the small little girl ~~that~~ *[who]* took my place will think of a way to escape when she is ready.	*The author writes a conclusion that sums up very well the goals the servant slave expressed earlier in the story.* *[W6.3.5, 7.3.5, 8.3.5]*

STORY #3: A Very Cute Intruder

STORY	COMMENTS
"Oh, how gross, Monkey. Come on - stop licking me!" said Molly as she opened her eyes. It was 2:30 in the morning and Monkey was trying to wake her up. ~~He looked scared and as soon as~~ Molly looked into his eyes [*; he looked scared and]* she knew that something was wrong.	*By looking into his eyes, that is how she knew he looked scared, so I moved looking scared AFTER looking into his eyes instead of before.* [*W6.3.1, 7.3.1, 8.3.1]* *It would be more logical if Monkey started growling and that is what woke Molly up. A growling, tough angry dog would give Molly the courage to go looking for the intruder; a mild mannered dog would not, in which case Molly would yell for her mother to confront the intruder.* [*W6.3.4, 7.3.4, 8.3.4]*
Suddenly she heard something fall in the living room. She thought there must be a stranger in the house because her mother would never wake up in the middle of the night.	*Author explains why Molly concluded that it must be a stranger making the noise.*
She got up and put her slippers on, got Monkey's metal chain from her bookshelf and called to Monkey "Lead the way Monk." Monkey got up and started to walk very slowly, sniffing the ground for anything unusual.	*It might be more logical for Monkey to have his ears cocked, listening for more sounds and/or sniffing the air for scents, not sniffing the floor, since the intruder had not gotten as far as the bedroom.*
When they reached the living room, Monkey stopped and looked back *[at Molly]* ~~and then Molly came towards him~~.	*If Molly had Monkey on a chain, she would have been standing right behind him and would not have to move closer.*
She scanned the living room to see if anyone was there, but there was no one in sight.	*Molly should be able to see what fell in the living room that woke her up. Problem: what could a small puppy knock over that would make that much noise?* *May be illogical. Maybe a rustling sound that woke Monkey up and that continued when Molly woke up would be more realistic.*

STORY	COMMENTS
Then BAM! A noise came from the kitchen! She walked ~~over towards~~ *[to]* the kitchen door, and with her hands trembling, slowly, quietly opened it.	*"hands trembling" indicates she is frightened.* *[W6.3.4, 7.3.4, 8.3.4]*
"Awe, your so cute!" she said "Ruff Ruff" barked Monkey. "Shut up Monkey! You're gonna wake up mom!" The intruder that Molly was so scared of was a small Golden Retriever puppy, the same breed as Monkey. It was one of the cutest animals that Molly had ever seen in her life.	*"in her life" is redundant; where else but in her life would she have seen it? Comment: Logic question - what could the puppy do to make a "Bam" sound?" The author should tell us.*
It looked hungry so Molly got some biscuits out of the pantry and placed some on the floor. Then she picked up the puppy and brought it to her room.	*At this point, instead of later, the author should have Molly figure out how the puppy got in (it was through the doggy door).* *Let her leave the puppy in the kitchen with Monkey so that they both make the mess that her mother finds when she comes into the kitchen the next morning.*
"OK Monkey, you have to take care of the puppy tonight and in the morning we have to somehow convince mom to keep it, got it?" Molly asked. "Ruff" he barked in reply, "Good. Now go to sleep."	*Going to sleep sets the stage for the mother's reaction when she wakes up the next morning, as described in the next paragraph.*
"AAAAHHHHHAHHHHAHAHHAHAHHA-HAH[!!]" Molly *[was so startled by her mother's shrill scream that she]* fell out of bed to the shrill scream of her mother. She ran to the kitchen where her mother was staring in disbelief. "Ma what happened?" she asked panting. Monkey walked into the kitchen and made a puppy face at Molly's mom.	*The preceding sentence is not necessary. If her mother was screaming from the kitchen, it is only logical that it is because she has discovered the unexpected presence of the puppy.*
"Molly, who is this?" Molly's mother said pointing at the puppy. Molly took a good look around the now destroyed kitchen *[The kitchen was a mess.]*	*Describe what the mess in the kitchen looked like.* *[W6.3.2, 7.3.2, 8.3.2]*

STORY	COMMENTS
"Please don't tell me that you went out and found yourself another dog, because we don't have any space in the house to keep this thing." "I didn't go and find the dog. It must have gotten got into the house through Monkey's doggy door!	*This would be logical, since the puppy could not get in through a window or could not open the regular door. Many people add a small swinging doggy door as part of their regular door.* *[W6.3.2, 7.3.2, 8.3.2]*
Last night at around 3:00 a.m. I heard a noise and I thought someone had broken into the house, and when I went to see who it was, I found this cute thing with its nose in Monkey's bowl, trying to get some food." she explained. "So what do we do now? Do you want me to keep it?" Mom asked. "Well my birthday is coming in five days, so this could be an early and only present." Molly said. " OK, that does make sense, but there are some rules. You have to keep one dog in the house and the other in the barn. If I were you I would raise the young one in the house, and when it gets older, keep both of them in the barn. Also, you have to do everything to take care of it; only bother me for food and necessary supplies. If you agree to follow these rules the dog is yours." said Molly's mother. Molly jumped up and gave her mother a big hug! Molly was so happy! "Thank you! Thank you! Thank you! Thank you so much! I'm gonna name her Maggi!"	*The author should explain why Molly will name her new puppy Maggi.* *[W6.3.4, 7.3.4, 8.3.4]*

STORY #4: The Choice

STORY	COMMENTS
BEEP! BEEP! BEEP! sounded the alarm clock in Andy's room. He woke up with a start and then he yelled "YESSSS." He leaped out of bed and began jumping up and down and shouting: "Today is the day, today is the day!"	*The author does a good job of communicating the excitement Andy feels, by using the words "YESSSS", "leaped", "jumping up and down" and "shouting."* *[L6.5.1, 7.5.1, 8.5.1]*
Andy's mother walked into the room "Wow cowboy, slow down there. Remember - the violin plays soothing music, not heavy metal!" She said. So with this hint So in response, Andy began to dance a ballet, and his mother began to laugh. "Okay, come on, brush your hair, shower, and come downstairs with your ~~bag~~ *[backpack]* for breakfast. Oh, and did you finish your homework last night?" his mother asked. ~~while she walked out the door~~. "Yes mom, all of it." Andy replied. "Be down in a flash." ~~and so he was~~.	*"while she walked out the door" and "and so he was" are unnecessary word in the story.* *[W6.3.1, 7.3.1, 8.3.1]*
Andy was in third grade and today was the day that Andy's class got to choose the [musical] instrument that they wanted to learn on for the rest of their school year. Ever since Andy knew that this day would come *[,]* he was set on learning the violin because that's what his grandmother used to play when she was his age. After *[quickly]* finishing a bowl of cereal, Andy rushed to the car. and sat down with his seatbelt fastened. "Mom, come on let's go! We're going to be late!" Andy screamed. "Andy, let Peter put his shoes on just one more minute!" *[Finally they drove off.]* Andy got his wish and they all were sitting in the car.	*Here again, the author communicates a sense of urgency by using the words "quickly," "rushed","let's go! We're going to be late!"* *[W6.3.1, 7.3.1, 8.3.1]* *[W6.3.4, 7.3.4, 8.3.4]*

STORY	COMMENTS
"Dad wished you good luck for the big day when he called this morning," Andy's mother said. "He also said that Ireland has a good luck pool where he put a coin for you." ~~Andy said really excited.~~	*There is no musical competition today, only the selection of an instrument, and every student gets to choose an instrument, so why does his father have to wish Andy luck? Luck with what? Illogical?*
Then Andy's mom parked the car. ~~and then all got down.~~ ~~As soon as~~ Andy ~~hit the ground with his Nike sneakers he~~ gave his mom a big hug and ran right straight for the door. As soon as he walked into the school he saw his music teacher, and he said "Good Morning Mrs. Musinca." "Oh Good Mooooorning Andy."	*"Moooorning" is an example of the intentional misspelling technique.* *[L6.5.1, 7.5.1, 8.5.1]*
"Are you ready to pick your instrument today?" the kind teacher asked. "Oh yes ma'am I have been waiting for a long time. I want to pick the violin." he said excitedly. Mrs. Musinca nodded, winked, then walked away. Then Andy heard the bell ring so he hurried off to his classroom. He stopped at the door where the sign 33 hung and peered inside to see if everyone had ~~come already~~ *[arrived ;]* there were still some empty seats and people were putting their backpacks away. He knew that he was on time so he walked in casually. The teacher, Mr. Gates, stood and said "Good Morning kids. Okay, you guys know the drill, let's say the Pledge of Allegiance," and then all of the kids ~~started "I pledge allegiance to the flag of the united states~~ ~~of America and to the republic for which it stands one~~ ~~nation under god, indivisible and with liberty and justice~~ ~~for all."~~ *[recited the Pledge.]*	*A semicolon used here to separate two sentences joined because they are closely related.* *I don't think printing the Pledge is necessary to the story.*
"Thank you students, you all are getting better day by day when it comes to saying the Pledge together as one voice."	

STORY	COMMENTS
"Um, what special class do we have today?" Mr. Gates asked. "WE HAVE MUSIC" They all chorused. "That's right! But first let's finish with our math and other subjects. Today we are going to work on Geometry. How many of you forgot to get your geo boards today?" questioned the teacher. None of the students raised their hands. "EXCELLENT!" Mr. Gates exclaimed. So the day went on like this and the students kept Mr. Gates in a very good mood. Soon enough the lunch bell rang; everyone had been waiting for this because right after the lunch period ~~the students would go to the music room~~! *[was the music period.]*	*Most of the preceding paragraph about math is not really necessary to the story. [W6.3.3, 7.3.3, 8.3.3]*
[After lunch,] all of the students *[in Mr. Gates classroom sat]* ~~of room 33 had finished their lunches very quickly and were~~ waiting for the bell to ring *[and]* ~~Once they heard that~~ *[the]* ~~bell ring they all got up and they were jumping up and down~~ for Mrs. Musinca to arrive. When she finally got there she had a big smile on her face."OKAY EVERYONE, LINE UP" she yelled, and at once all of the students lined up in single file. She then gave the command "FORWARD MARCH" and twenty pairs of small legs marched to the music room *[very excited]*. ~~As soon as they walked into the room, they were all very excited but made sure that they stayed in the line only because it was one of the 'must follow rules' in the class room. 'Never fall out of line until told to.'~~	*Notice how many words have strikethrough lines through them. These words are no needed and do not add anything important to the story.*
Mrs. Musinca went to her desk and pulled out an attendance sheet. ~~"Now each student will be called one by one and he or she will tell me what they want to play from the spot where they are standing now. You have to give me your choice from the list that is behind you, and make sure that it is there.~~	*The preceding sentence is in the passive voice and is too wordy. Here is how it would appear if the active voice were used: "I will call each of your names, and you will tell me which instrument you are choosing,selected from the list posted behind you." The active voice format says the same thing but uses fewer words.*

STORY	COMMENTS
Then the calling began, "Andrew" she called "The cello" he replied. "Marvelous choice." She said. "Andy" she called "Violin." he replied cheerfully. "A high spirited instrument for a high spirited boy." she said. After the last name was called, the students calling went on and on and then in the end a boy named Zang was called and he picked the saxophone and then they all were very anxious to see what their teacher would do.Then She said "Well, what now. Hmmmmm I think that I am going to give you all a little time to examine the instruments that you have chosen. The school has rented many instruments for you as the parents instructed. So you may look at the instrument that they have gotten you and then you can take it home when you have brought the money for this year." Then with a nod from every one she called all of the names and told them to come forth while handing them the right instrument and size that was ordered for them.	*There is a problem with the logic here. In a previous paragraph, the teacher says to the students "you will tell me which instrument you are choosing, selected from the list posted behind you.". But in the preceding paragraph, it sounds like the parents were the ones who selected each instrument for their son or daughter. The author has to rewrite this to make it clear which statement is the correct one.*
She called Andrew, and he went to her desk, and Mrs. Musinca wrote his name on a tag and tied it to the handle of a violin case. Then she held it out and said: "Take care of it, Andy. It is really special."	
WHOLE STORY	*[W6.3.1, 7.3.1, 8.3.1]*

STORY #5: A Stressful Change

STORY	COMMENTS
It was a fine August afternoon and fall would soon be closing in on the small town of Piscataway. Lyra Robinson and her parents had landed at JFK International airport after a very long flight from Australia. Lyra was going into 4th grade. She wasn't so excited about this move, but it came about because Lyra's father had been promoted to team leader at a company called American Standards. Lyra was proud of her dad for getting a job here but she was upset that they had to move just for the job. Eventually her mother got her to understand that if they didn't move, they would be away from daddy for a very long time. So, reluctantly, she accepted the necessity for the move, and here they were in a taxicab heading from the airport to their newly purchased house.	*Good introductory paragraph. It introduces Lyra, the main character, and tells the reader where she is coming from, where she is going to live now, why she is making a move, what her attitude is and the fact that Lyra will be going into fourth grade.* *[W6.3.1, 7.3.1, 8.3.1]* *[W6.3.4, 7.3.4, 8.3.4]*
THUD! THUD! The taxi went over a speed bump and woke her from a deep sleep. "Lyra dearie, welcome to our new home!" her mother said in an excited voice. As much as Lyra did not like to admit it, the house was beautiful, full of greenery around it, and on the door was the bold golden number 23.Lyra looked at her watch and it was already 10:00 in the morning. She *[looked around the street and]* said in a frantic voice: "Mum, Mum where are all of the kids here? I don't see anyone riding bikes or doing anything. It looks so boring; it looks like it's a place for old people to hang out." She cried "Now now Lyra, you must not judge a place by the first look, okay? Now lets go inside the house and start unpacking." Then her mother turned back to see Lyra's father sleeping as well. "Well am I the only one who didn't sleep in the car? Jim wake up now!" She yelled. "Mary what is it?" Jim said. "We reached the house Jim. Look at it, so beautiful." Then her father got up and said, "Okay, come on out of the car, we got a big day ahead of us, lets go go go!".	*[W6.3.2, 7.3.2, 8.3.2]* *[W6.3.4, 7.3.4, 8.3.4]*

STORY	COMMENTS
Her parents' comments ignited a happy spirit inside Lyra. The Robinsons were ready to do anything today. Lyra jumped out of the car to feel the sun on her face; it was such a beautiful place to live in. Lyra had imagined that the place would be like a dump, but now she could see it was bigger and better than the small apartment they had back in Australia. Then there was a huge sound in behind her Then she heard the loud sound of a trailer truck engine and airbrakes. When she turned around there was a huge 18 wheel tractor trailer truck that had just pulled up to their house. With the sound of the brakes finally ending Lyra's father went over to the back waiting for the driver to come and open the door for him. By the time that the truck driver had opened all of the locks on the truck's loading doors, Lyra's mom had opened the front door and the garage doors. Soon all of the boxes were being carried toward the house. Lyra was so bored that she started to help her mother. They both worked together to open everything from the plastic wrap and make sure that nothing was broken, especially the collection of little handmade dolls that were made by Lyra's mother.	
By the time it was 3:00 in the afternoon, Lyra was worn out and asked her mom to make some lunch. The only problem was, they didn't know where to call for restaurants or delis that would deliver, which they needed since they did not have a car. Then Lyra's mother got an idea. "Hey why don't we go and ask one of our neighbors. They might know some place where we could get some food, right?" she asked. "Of course we would" said a voice at the front door. There were two adults and two kids; one of the children looked very small and was very adorable. "Why yes you did, so let me guess - you are from Australia right?" Meena asked. "Rightiyo" said Jim. "Well I couldn't help but overhear - you guys are having some trouble with ordering lunch, right? Well how about we take you out for lunch, and please don't say no. It is our way of welcoming you to the town," said Meena.	*[W6.3.3, 7.3.3, 8.3.3]* *[W6.3.1, 7.3.1, 8.3.1]*

STORY	COMMENTS
"Oh thank you so much - yes I think that we would like to have some lunch, and we would be able to get to know you too." said Mary. So Lyra and her parents went out to lunch with their new neighbors. They were very nice people and Lyra liked them a lot. The rest of the day went smoothly and they were able to unpack almost everything. Then Lyra remembered that she had school tomorrow, and suddenly she became worried about what was going to happen then. But the only thing she could do was wait.	*The author mentioned that Kavin, one of the new neighbor's children, was Lyra's age. She could have asked Kavin about the school; she did end up riding on the school bus with him the next morning. [W6.3.3, 7.3.3, 8.3.3]*
The next day, Lyra woke up at six o'clock and got ready for school. Her mother had packed her favorite food, pasta with some cilantro on top. She went to the bus stop with her father. The school bus came. "Okay darling, now be good in school, got it?" her father asked. Lyra nodded 'yes', gave him a hug and then ran for the bus. When she got on the bus *[she saw]* there were all these friendly faces smiling at her, looking eager to become friends with her. She then remembered that Kavin was also going to be on the same bus, so she looked for him and when he came right behind her, he said: "Hey Lyra, move back so we can sit together." She smiled and then ~~the two new friends moved over to the~~ *[both of them moved to the]* back of the bus. Then the bus started to move and all of the students on the bus were chatting with their friends and rejoicing after two months of holidays – everyone, that is, except for Lyra; she was worried about what school would be like for her.	
Once they reached the school Kavin led Lyra to classroom 27 and then said bye and went to. his own classroom. From here on it was going to be Lyra on her own. She took a deep breath and then she took one step into the classroom.	

STORY	COMMENTS
She was surprised at how happy the kids were*[; it made her feel more relaxed.]* ~~and the jolly feeling that she got as soon as she walked into the room~~. Then someone tapped her on the back and said "Excusem Moi." She turned around to see the smiling face of her teacher. "You must be Lyra, am I right?" she asked. Lyra nodded shyly. "My name is Mrs. Hutchinson, how are you today?" "I am fine Mrs. Hutchinson." Lyra said. Mrs. Hutchinson went to her desk, and said "Good morning students!" The whole room fell silent, but then they all said "Good Morning Mrs Hutchinson!" followed by the Pledge of Allegiance. Lyra didn't know the Pledge, so she just stood with her right hand on her heart. Then they all sat down and then Mrs. Hutchinson stood up. "Today I am seeing many familiar faces, but I don't know your names, so let's start by introducing ourselves, starting with I think it best for us to start from the newest member of our school, Lyra. She is the pretty little girl sitting right over there. Sweetie, stand up and say your name and where you are from; the rest of you can just say your names." Lyra said. "Hi, um my name is Lyra and I am from Australia." For some reason everyone clapped and then she sat down. By the time all 28 students had said their names, Lyra had memorized their faces and first names. Once the introductions were done, the teacher didn't start with the lessons; instead, she passed out folders and then she showed the students where everything was in the school.	*explain what was in the folders* *We have to assume that the school was new to all the other classmates of Lyra's, that they were all coming from another building that had housed the third grade, otherwise, why would this teacher have to show them around the school?* *[W6.3.2, 7.3.2, 8.3.2]*
When they got back to the classroom she showed them where all the books should be kept and how the classroom should be utilized. Lyra was very happy throughout the day, especially while she was eating lunch with her new friends Rajeena and Trudy. They were really nice and were on Lyra's bus.	

STORY	COMMENTS
Time flew by and Lyra was so busy and enjoying school that she didn't even realize when it was time to go home. She said bye to Mrs. Hutchinson and then she called over to Trudy and Rajeena, and they both walked with her to their bus. It was a fun day for Lyra and she just couldn't wait to tell her mom what had happened. about her first day at school.	*The events in the story follow a timeline that the author makes very clear, starting with the arrival at the new house in the afternoon, then a late lunch with the new neighbors, then bedtime, then the next morning going to school, the lunch period, and the end of the school day. The author also describes Lyra's feelings during the story. The author provides detailed descriptions of the events in the story.* *[W6.3.3, 7.3.3, 8.3.3]*

STORY #6: The Night Before Christmas

STORY	COMMENTS
It was Christmas eve, the twenty fourth of December, and Ron was looking at the night sky from the balcony of his room. He could hear the fire crackling in the hearth while he was staring at the twinkling blanket of stars above him. There was a slight breeze, which made him realize that it was a bit too cold for him to watch the twinkling sky much longer.	*The author does a nice job of describing the setting – fire crackling, twinkling blanket of stars (a metaphor), twinkling sky - and the time period of Christmas eve.* *[W6.3.1, 7.3.1, 8.3.1]* *[W.6.4, 7.3.4, 8.3.4]*
He walked ~~into~~ *[through his]* ~~the~~ room and went ~~to~~ *[into]* the hall *[and saw]* ~~to see~~ that his children, Anna and Jacob, were still awake, and were helping his wife Roseina decorate their lovely Christmas tree. He took a few steps down the hall and then he saw *[a piece of]* paper that was lying on the ~~stair's~~ *[staircase]* landing. ~~The piece of paper revealed to be~~ *[It was]* a photo of Ron's family all having fun and putting up their Christmas tree on Christmas Eve. Ron slowly walked back to his room and sank into his bed, still holding the photo *[and]* remembering that day so many years ago so vividly that it was almost as if it was going on right in front of his eyes.	*"revealed to be" is much too pretentious and wordy; just say it "was"* *The phrase "so many years ago" is a trigger; it signals the reader that this is the beginning of a flashback, even though the reader might have figured this out already.* *[L6.5.1, 7.5.1, 8.5.1]*
"Ronny be careful with that sweetie; it is made of glass and it might brake [break]" said Ron's mother. "Okay mom, I won't ~~brake~~ *[break]* it. But what is it? It looks like two birds with the same body." Ron said. "How can two birds have the same body? That's not possible" said Mareena, Ron's older sister. "It doesn't look that way to me; I think they just made it look like that so they could sell the ornament as one whole piece." said Ron's older brother Johnny.	

STORY	COMMENTS
Then their mother said: "Ronny is right; on this matter the two heads represent two doves or two friends and the one body ~~says~~ *[means]* that they are always friends and that they are connected through a special bond that will never break or die." She stopped *[, smiled, and]* ~~with a smile then~~ looked at all of them. "It can be compared to the bond between brothers and sisters and *[means that]* even if they fight and have rough times, they will always stay together. That is the way that I want all of you to be. No matter what comes your way, you all have to stand together."	*"says" indicates speech, and the body is not speaking, so use "means" instead of says. the flashback is ending and the story is returning to its original time and place from which the story began.*
[Ron's imaginary trip into the past ended when] suddenly Roseina came into the room, "Whatya got there?" She came across the room and took the photo from Ron's hand. She *[looked at]* ~~saw~~ it and smiled. *[She said: "]* Whenever I look at this photo I remember my childhood and how I used to put up the tree with my mother ~~when I was little~~.	*"Ron's imaginary trip into the past ended" is a trigger that alerts the reader that the flashback is ending and the story is returning to its original time and place from which the story began.* *Childhood implies that you were little.* *[L6.5.1, 7.5.1, 8.5.1]*
Time flies *[by]* so fast that I still feel like it was yesterday when I was putting up the tree with the help of my brothers, and now I am putting up a tree with my own children." Ron just smiled and was thinking the same thing. Then she gave him a hug and said "Come downstairs; we need your help in putting the star on the top of the tree." ~~Then~~ Ron got up and said "Let's go !"	*[L6.5.1, 7.5.1, 8.5.1]*

STORY #7: A Day in a Life of Conackamack Middle School

STORY	COMMENTS
"RRRRRRRIIIIIIIIIIIINNNNNNNNGGGGGGG" went the bell at the end of 3rd period. I walked out of class thinking ~~what I had next period~~ *[about my next class --]* MATH ! -- my least favorite subject! What was I going to do this time to occupy myself during class? During my last math class I ate my lunch and then bought something else during lunch break and then the class before that I took Ruchit's phone and started to play Angry Birds. Today Ruchit is absent and mom gave me some money to buy lunch in the cafeteria because she is sick, but I bought something and ate it already, so all I can do to pass the time in Math class is daydream.	*This is an example of intentional misspelling and onomatopoeia.* *[L6.5.1, 7.5.1, 8.5.1]* *[W6.1.3, 7.1.3, 8.1.3]*
~~I sat for~~ *[During]* the first five minutes of the class Mr. Hickson's voice was so droopy that I was dozing off in my chair, as hard as I tried not to. Eventually my partner and the person sitting in front of me both fell asleep. Then I remembered that last night I stayed up late studying for the English test that I had this morning. That is why I am feeling so tired! Maybe it won't hurt to rest my eyes for a little bit. But the second I closed my eyes I was in a deep sleep that I thought no one except for my mom and her raging voice could bring me out of. After a few minutes of being asleep *[I began to]* the dream started.	*"the dream started" is passive voice; prior to this the author used active voices, for example "I closed, I thought", so to be consistent, use "I began to" instead of "the dream started.", "I began to dream" is a trigger that will transport the reader into the dream, which is the story within the story.* *[L6.5.1, 7.5.1, 8.5.1]*
It was very dark and the only thing that was visible was a chalkboard and the walls of a room that looked very familiar to me. It was my math classroom*[;]* and then suddenly there was the math teacher who appeared out of thin air.	

STORY	COMMENTS
"Well, well Hickson, looks like you decided to show up after all, didn't you" someone said. To my surprise it was me who was talking so rudely to my math teacher, but I wasn't frightened. I let the dream continue in my mind	*Dreams can only take place in one's mind, so the phrase "in my mind" is redundant.*
"I am sorry that I am late sir, I was brushing my teeth." he said in a frightful voice.	*"fearful" is a better adjective to use*
"That is no excuse, Hickson," I said. "You know that the rule says: 'If you are more than five minutes late to class, I have to send you to the Assistant Principal's office.' So, when this class ends, you are to go there, and here is the slip he will sign that you will return to me showing that you actually went." "But, but, that is not fair! I object! You have no right..." he shouted.	
"I guess you also forgot that you are not to argue with your teacher. Because you did, I am assigning you a math problem that you need to solve and give me the answer after your next study period today." I said. "No, I won't do it. Math is so boring the way you teach it." he said.	
"Yes, you will do it or I'll give you detention. Here is the problem, write it down: Take the square root of 45, and to it add 2.5 to the fifth power, and to that add 16.3 divided by .043, and write out the answer".Suddenly I woke up. Delightfully I found that the classroom was still very bright. The bell rang and as I was walking outside. I thought that the dream was actually quite a satisfying one.	*"suddenly woke up" is the trigger that brings the reader back from the main character's daydream to the original setting in the classroom.* *Unlike a flashback, the daydream took place in the present, at the same time the character was in the class.*

The stories in this chapter are examples of:

Writing: W.6.1,6.3,7.1,7.3,8.1,8.3.

Language: L.6.1,6.2,6.3,6.5,7.1,7.2,7.3,7.5,8.1,8.2,8.3,8.5.

Chapter XIV :
Common Core State Standards Initiative
(CCSSI) Standards for Writing and Language

Editor's Notes:

1. Only those standards that relate to the exercises in this workbook are listed here.

2. Any part of a CCSS standard listed here to which none of the exercises in these workshops relate has been omitted or replaced with ... to indicate omitted language.

3. Format: W=writing, L= language; next is grade; last is paragraph number.

English Language Arts Standards: Writing

Grade 6: Text Types and Purposes

Standard	Description	Page Nos.
W.6.1.	Write arguments to support claims with clear reasons and relevant evidence. 1. Introduce claim(s) and organize the reasons and evidence clearly. 2. Support claim(s) with clear reasons and relevant evidence, using credible sources and demonstrating an understanding of the topic or text. 3. Use words, phrases, and clauses to clarify the relationships among claim(s) and reasons. 4. Establish and maintain a formal style. 5. Provide a concluding statement or section that follows from the argument presented	43 54 83 113 114
W.6.2.	Write informative/explanatory texts to examine a topic and convey ideas, concepts, and information through the selection, organization, and analysis of relevant content. 1. Introduce a topic clearly, previewing what is to follow; organize ideas, concepts, and information, using strategies such as definition, classification, comparison/contrast, and cause/effect; include formatting (e.g., headings), graphics (e.g., charts, tables), and multimedia when useful to aiding comprehension. 2. Develop the topic with relevant facts, definitions, concrete details, quotations, or other information and examples. 3. Use appropriate transitions to create cohesion and clarify the relationships among ideas and concepts. 4. Use precise language and domain-specific vocabulary to inform about or explain the topic.	54

Grade 6: Text Types and Purposes

Standard	Description	Page Nos.
W.6.2.	5. Establish and maintain a formal style. 6. Provide a concluding statement or section that follows from and supports the information or explanation presented.	
W.6.3.	Write narratives to develop real or imagined experiences or events using effective technique, relevant descriptive details, and well-structured event sequences. 1. Engage and orient the reader by establishing a context and introducing a narrator and/or characters; organize an event sequence that unfolds naturally and logically. 2. Use narrative techniques, such as dialogue, pacing, and description, to develop experiences, events, and/or characters. 3. Use a variety of transition words, phrases, and clauses to convey sequence and signal shifts from one time frame or setting to another. 4. Use precise words and phrases, relevant descriptive details, and sensory language to capture the action and convey experiences and events. 5. Provide a conclusion that follows from and reflects on the narrated experiences or events.	2, 24, 26, 35, 41, 48, 83, 87, 88, 89, 90, 91, 92, 93, 94, 95, 96, 97, 98, 99, 100,101, 102,104, 105,106, 107,109, 110,111, 114

Grade 7: Text Types and Purposes

Standard	Description	Page Nos.
W.7.1.	Write arguments to support claims with clear reasons and relevant evidence. 1. Introduce claim(s), acknowledge and distinguish the claim(s) from alternate or opposing claims, and organize the reasons and evidence logically. 2. Support claim(s) with logical reasoning and relevant evidence, using accurate, credible sources and demonstrating an understanding of the topic or text. 3. Use words, phrases, and clauses to create cohesion and clarify the relationships among claim(s), counterclaims, reasons, and evidence. 4. Establish and maintain a formal style. 5. Provide a concluding statement or section that follows from and supports the argument presented.	43, 50, 54, 83, 113

Grade 7: Text Types and Purposes

Standard	Description	Page Nos.
W.7.2	Write informative/explanatory texts to examine a topic and convey ideas, concepts, and information through the selection, organization, and analysis of relevant content. 1. Introduce a topic clearly, previewing what is to follow; organize ideas, concepts, and information, using strategies such as definition, classification, comparison/contrast, and cause/effect; include formatting (e.g., headings), graphics (e.g., charts, tables), and multimedia when useful to aiding comprehension. 2. Develop the topic with relevant facts, definitions, concrete details, quotations, or other information and examples. 3. Use appropriate transitions to create cohesion and clarify the relationships among ideas and concepts. 4. Use precise language and domain-specific vocabulary to inform about or explain the topic. 5. Establish and maintain a formal style. 6. Provide a concluding statement or section that follows from and supports the information or explanation presented.	50, 54
W.7.3	Write narratives to develop real or imagined experiences or events using effective technique, relevant descriptive details, and well-structured event sequences. 1. Engage and orient the reader by establishing a context and point of view and introducing a narrator and/or characters; organize an event sequence that unfolds naturally and logically. 2. Use narrative techniques, such as dialogue, pacing, and description, to develop experiences, events, and/or characters. 3. Use a variety of transition words, phrases, and clauses to convey sequence and signal shifts from one time frame or setting to another. 4. Use precise words and phrases, relevant descriptive details, and sensory language to capture the action and convey experiences and events. 5. Provide a conclusion that follows from and reflects on the narrated experiences or events.	24, 26, 41, 83, 87, 88, 89,90, 91, 94, 95, 96, 97, 98, 99,100, 101, 102, 104, 105, 106, 107, 108, 109, 110, 111

Grade 8: Text Types and Purposes

Standard	Description	Page Nos.
W.8.1.	Write arguments to support claims with clear reasons and relevant evidence. 1. Introduce claim(s), acknowledge and distinguish the claim(s) from alternate or opposing claims, and organize the reasons and evidence logically. 2. Support claim(s) with logical reasoning and relevant evidence, using accurate, credible sources and demonstrating an understanding of the topic or text. 3. Use words, phrases, and clauses to create cohesion and clarify the relationships among claim(s), counterclaims, reasons, and evidence. 4. Establish and maintain a formal style. 5. Provide a concluding statement or section that follows from and supports the argument presented.	43, 54, 83, 113
W.8.2.	Write informative/explanatory texts to examine a topic and convey ideas, concepts, and information through the selection, organization, and analysis of relevant content. 1. Introduce a topic clearly, previewing what is to follow; organize ideas, concepts, and information into broader categories; include formatting (e.g., headings), graphics (e.g., charts, tables), and multimedia when useful to aiding comprehension. 2. Develop the topic with relevant, well-chosen facts, definitions, concrete details, quotations, or other information and examples. 3. Use appropriate and varied transitions to create cohesion and clarify the relationships among ideas and concepts. 4. Use precise language and domain-specific vocabulary to inform about or explain the topic. 5. Establish and maintain a formal style. 6. Provide a concluding statement or section that follows from and supports the information or explanation presented.	54
W.8.3.	Write narratives to develop real or imagined experiences or events using effective technique, relevant descriptive details, and well-structured event sequences.	

Grade 8: Text Types and Purposes		
Standard	Description	Page Nos.
W.8.3.	Introduce claim(s), acknowledge and distinguish the claim(s) from alternate or opposing claims, and organize the reasons and evidence logically. 1. Engage and orient the reader by establishing a context and point of view and introducing a narrator and/or characters; organize an event sequence that unfolds naturally and logically. 2. Use narrative techniques, such as dialogue, pacing, description, and reflection, to develop experiences, events, and/or characters. 3. Use a variety of transition words, phrases, and clauses to convey sequence, signal shifts from one time frame or setting to another and show the relationships among experiences and events. 4. Use precise words and phrases, relevant descriptive details, and sensory language to capture the action and convey experiences and events. 5. Provide a conclusion that follows from and reflects on the narrated experiences or events.	24, 26, 41, 83, 87, 88, 89, 90, 91, 92, 93, 94, 95, 96, 97, 98, 99, 100, 101, 102, 104, 105, 106, 107, 108, 109, 110, 111

English Language Arts Standards: Language

	Grade 6 Conventions of Standard English	

Standard	Description	Page Nos.
L.6.1	Demonstrate command of the conventions of standard English grammar and usage when writing or speaking. 1. Ensure that pronouns are in the proper case (subjective, objective, possessive). 2. Recognize variations from standard English in their own and others' writing and speaking, and identify and use strategies to improve expression in conventional language.	24, 83
L.6.2	Demonstrate command of the conventions of standard English capitalization, punctuation, and spelling when writing. 1. Use punctuation (commas, parentheses, dashes) to set off nonrestrictive/ parenthetical elements. 2. Spell correctly.	83
Knowledge of Language		
L.6.3.	Use knowledge of language and its conventions when writing, speaking, reading, or listening. 1. Vary sentence patterns for meaning, reader/listener interest, and style. 2. Maintain consistency in style and tone.	83
Vocabulary Acquisition and Use		
L.6.5.	Demonstrate understanding of figurative language, word relationships, and nuances in word meanings. 1. Interpret figures of speech (e.g., personification) in context.	20, 28, 35, 38, 83, 87,102, 103, 111, 112,113

Grade 7: Conventions of Standard English

Standard	Description	Page Nos.
L.7.1	Demonstrate command of the conventions of standard English grammar and usage when writing or speaking.	24, 83, 114
L.7.2.	Demonstrate command of the conventions of standard English capitalization, punctuation, and spelling when writing. 1. Spell correctly.	83, 114
Knowledge of Language		
L.7.3.	Use knowledge of language and its conventions when writing, speaking, reading, or listening. 1. Choose language that expresses ideas precisely and concisely, recognizing and eliminating wordiness and redundancy.	20, 83, 114
Vocabulary Acquisition and Use		
L.7.5.	Demonstrate understanding of figurative language, word relationships, and nuances in word meanings. 1. Interpret figures of speech (e.g., literary, biblical, and mythological allusions) in context.	20, 28, 35, 38, 83, 87,102, 103,111, 112,113, 114

Grade 8: Conventions of Standard English

Standard	Description	Page Nos.
L.8.1	Demonstrate command of the conventions of standard English grammar and usage when writing or speaking. 1. Form and use verbs in the active and passive voice. 2. Recognize and correct inappropriate shifts in verb voice and mood.	24, 83, 114

Grade 8: Conventions of Standard English

Standard	Description	Page Nos.
L.8.2	Demonstrate command of the conventions of standard English capitalization, punctuation, and spelling when writing. 1. Use punctuation (comma, ellipsis, dash) to indicate a pause or break. 2. Spell correctly.	83,114
Knowledge of Language		
L.8.3.	Use knowledge of language and its conventions when writing, speaking, reading, or listening. 1. Use verbs in the active and passive voice and in the conditional and subjunctive mood to achieve particular effects (e.g., emphasizing the actor or the action; expressing uncertainty or describing a state contrary to fact).	83,114
Vocabulary Acquisition and Use		
L.8.5.	Demonstrate understanding of figurative language, word relationships, and nuances in word meanings. 1. Interpret figures of speech (e.g. verbal irony, puns) in context.	20, 28, 35, 38, 83, 87, 102,103, 111, 112, 113, 114

Chapter XV
Grading Rubrics For Exercises In Chapter I

Story Idea #1: A Boat And Its Journey

W.6.3., W.7.3 and W.8.3. Write narratives to develop real or imagined experiences or events using effective technique, relevant descriptive details, and well-structured event sequences.

1. Engage and orient the reader by establishing a context and point of view and introducing a narrator and/or characters; organize an event sequence that unfolds naturally and logically.

Rubric: Add points for additional characters added to the story idea. For example, the student could add details about the family that owned the boat, and about the family of the girl into whose dock the boat drifted. The student could also add details about living and nonliving characters that the boat encounters on its journey down the river.

2. Use narrative techniques, such as dialogue, pacing, description and reflection, to develop experiences, events, and/or characters.

Rubric: Dialogue can be added by personifying the boat and any non-human character it encounters. Dialogue can also be added between the little girl who sees the boat drifting into her dock and her family. Add points for additional descriptive details about the setting. For example, rock ledges in the river, or a surging tide, or details of the storm that broke the mooring line.

3. Use a variety of transition words, phrases, and clauses to convey sequence and signal shifts from one time frame or setting to another and show the relationships among experiences and events.

Rubric: The student can describe the passage of time during the boat's journey by describing the approaching evening and night and next morning, and details about the setting as it changes as the boat drifts down the river.

4. Use precise words and phrases, relevant descriptive details, and sensory language to convey experiences and events and capture the action.

Rubric: Sensory language can be used to describe the fear that the boat feels when the storm breaks its mooring line and casts it adrift, or its feelings when it encounters living or nonliving things in the river, which can bring feelings of comfort or rejection, depending on the dialogue and actions of these things. Points should be given when a student describes the feelings so that the reader concludes what they are rather than the student telegraphing them by using single words such as happy, sad, angry.

Points should be given for details that are relevant to the story and not extraneous. For example, details about the little girl's life – she always wanted to have a boat – are relevant.

5. Provide a conclusion that follows from and reflects on the narrated experiences or events.

Rubric: Points should be given if the story has a logical ending e.g. the girl takes some action relative to the boat that is drifting in to her dock. For example, she and her father could seek out the owners and return the boat to them, or adopt it as their own.

6. Additional points: for answering Assignment Questions 1-4.

Story Idea #2: An Amazing Chicken

W.6.3., **W.7.3** and **W.8.3**. Write narratives to develop real or imagined experiences or events using effective technique, relevant descriptive details, and well-structured event sequences.

1. Engage and orient the reader by establishing a context and point of view and introducing a narrator and/or characters; organize an event sequence that unfolds naturally and logically.

Rubric: Add points if the author establishes the context of the story in the introduction.

For example, describing the family and the ranchette and then narrowing the reader's focus by making it clear that the story is primarily focused on one of the animals – a hen.

Add points for adding characters, in addition to the hen, to the story idea.

For example, instead of a narrator telling the story, let the characters (the chicken herself, family members and/or other animals) tell it.

Events could be sequenced over time as Spike grows from a chick to an adult; otherwise, the only role for sequencing is to describe individual actions within an event in the order in which they happen.

A point of view could be to point out through Spike's activities how intelligent an animal can actually to counter a stereotype that most chickens are stupid and uninteresting.

2. Use narrative techniques, such as dialogue, pacing, description and reflection, to develop experiences, events, and/or characters.

Rubric: Dialogue can be added by personifying the chicken and the other animals so that they can tell stories about Spike, in addition to having family members tell stories about Spike. Add points for additional descriptive details about Spike's interactions with the other animals and members of the family.

3. Use a variety of transition words, phrases, and clauses to convey sequence and signal shifts from one time frame or setting to another and show the relationships among experiences and events.

Rubric: An author can describe the passage of time if events relating to Spike are sequenced over Spike's life cycle, or during a 24 hour period. For example, Spike may perform certain actions in the morning (ex. crowing like a rooster, making the rounds to visit the other animals) and other actions in the evening (coming into the house and joining the family as they watch TV programs).

4. Use precise words and phrases, relevant descriptive details, and sensory language to convey experiences and events and capture the action.

Rubric: Relevant descriptive detail could describe how the hen got an unusual name, or actions that she takes. Sensory language can be used to describe how family members felt about the hen, or how the hen reacted to sensory stimuli, such as being stroked (she fell asleep).

Points should be given when a student describes a character's feelings not by using single word adjectives such as happy, sad or angry, but by describing physical attributes or actions or spoken words in such a way that the reader concludes what the emotion is rather than the author telegraphing the emotion.

5. Provide a conclusion that follows from and reflects on the narrated experiences or events.

Rubric: May be difficult to meet this requirement. A story about this chicken's exploits may not lead to a conclusion or any reflections other than the point of view example given in paragraph 1 above.

6. Additional points should be given for answering Assignment Questions 1-4.

Rubric: The Narrative and/or Descriptive writing style is the most logical for this story idea, although Expository could be used in describing phenomena such as the hen warning the family when a female goat was having trouble delivering her baby. Persuasive could be used to try and convince the reader that a hen can be very intelligent.

<u>Story Idea #3:</u> The Boy From Africa

W.6.3., W.7.3 and W.8.3. Write narratives to develop real or imagined experiences or events using effective technique, relevant descriptive details, and well-structured event sequences.

1. Engage and orient the reader by establishing a context and point of view and introducing a narrator and/or characters; organize an event sequence that unfolds naturally and logically.

Rubric: Add points for adding events such as the teacher visiting a village in Liberia, and as a result, sponsoring a campaign in her school district to collect and send needed supplies there, and for adopting a child and bringing the child to her home and school.

Add points for an author who describes what it might be like for a child from a primitive village (no running water, no indoor plumbing, a very different diet from ours) to be placed in one of our schools.

Add points for an author who includes the reactions and comments by fellow students about the newcomer, and the feelings of the transplanted child. The events mentioned and the sequence in which they are listed (over a time period) in this paragraph are examples of a sequence "that unfolds naturally and logically," as described in the standard above.

Add points if the author adds his/her point of view or that of any character about the events in this story.

2. Use narrative techniques, such as dialogue, pacing, description and reflection, to develop experiences, events, and/or characters.

Rubric: There are many opportunities for dialogue between and among the teacher and the African villagers, the teacher and members of her school and community (relating to the collection and donation of supplies), and fellow students with the transplanted child.

Add points for the author's reflections on, for example, the meaning of this teacher's efforts and any other positive outcomes from the teacher's actions, and/or the actions of the community and classmates. This may coincide with any points of view as described in Paragraph 1 above.

Also, events such as those listed in Paragraph 1 above may meet the standards requirement "to develop experiences, events, and/or characters."

3. Use a variety of transition words, phrases, and clauses to convey sequence and signal shifts from one time frame or setting to another and show the relationships among experiences and events.

Rubric: Add points if the student includes more than one timeframe. In the examples of events listed above, the time frame could change from when the teacher makes her decision to do something for native Liberians to the collecting of supplies to the delivery of the supplies to the adoption of the child to the entry of the child into the American school. Corresponding to these changes in time are the changes in settings from the teacher's home town and school to a Liberian village and back to the home town and school.

4. Use precise words and phrases, relevant descriptive details, and sensory language to convey experiences and events and capture the action.

Rubric: Sensory language can be used to describe the feelings of the teacher toward the Liberian villages, toward the project to gather supplies, to her visit to Liberia, to the adoption process and to entering the child into a local school. Also, the author can include the feelings of others in the story, such as the African villagers, the community, and the child's classmates.

Points should be given when a student describes the feelings of these characters in a way that the reader concludes what they are rather than the student telegraphing them by using single words such as happy, sad, angry.

Points should be given for details that are relevant to the story and not extraneous.

5. Provide a conclusion that follows from and reflects on the narrated experiences or events.

Rubric: Points should be given if the story has a logical ending e.g. the child is enrolled in the local school and his or her transition is working out satisfactorily. Also, for any reflections/opinions/points of view expressed by the author.

6. Additional points: for answering Assignment Questions 1-4.

Rubric: A combination of the Narrative and/or Descriptive and Expository writing styles are the most logical for this story idea. Expository could be used to describe what life in a primitive Liberian village is like or what obstacles the transplanted child would face.

Online Resources

Visit Us Online

Visit our website to learn more about our company, teachers, products and services.

LumosLearning.com/quilldemo

Lumos Quill

Create custom interactive lessons and assessments that supplement classroom learning.

QuillPad.org

Quillpad

FREE Resource: Help Your Students Write Better Stories and Essays

Lumos Online Store

Request a cost proposal or purchase securely on our website

LumosLearning.com/store

CPSIA information can be obtained
at www.ICGtesting.com
Printed in the USA
BVHW011054260420
578540BV00014B/548